Road to Recovery
To L and Back

Cary John Efurd

To L and Back
By Cary John Efurd

Copyright © 2021
All rights reserved.

First Printing

Published by Cary Efurd
CaryEfurd@gmail.com

Cary John Efurd

Cary John Efurd and his wife, Debby, are the owners and operators of Efurd Homestead LLC, a 75-acre farm located three miles south of Pittsburg, Texas. They retired in 2017 from corporate careers in the Dallas, Texas, area. They now operate Efurd Homestead Airbnb vacation rentals and The Grass Cutters lawncare service. They raise purebred Red Brangus cattle and produce hay as a cash crop. Debby is the author of *Go Tell It*, available on Amazon.

Cary and Debby live through the peaks and valleys of life with Jesus Christ at the center of their marriage. They are passionate about their faith. Their stories of recovery and redemption are inspirational and have helped many people find hope in Jesus Christ.

Cary and Debby were married in 1988 and have three children and six grandchildren.

Welcome

I know it's typical to present history in chronological order, but this book isn't about history. It's to reveal how my life was miraculously changed, so each chapter is presented as I thought of their importance. Choose from the Table of Contents or just open the book to any page and read about my recovery from all kinds of difficulties.

My constant struggle with alcohol, mental illness, and many kinds of worries was exchanged for a better life—The Way of Jesus Christ. There is no fooling around with something this important. Read with sadness and gladness about the polar opposites in my journey—from out-of-control to a life worth living.

You don't have to think, as I did, that you are the worst person living on Earth. You or someone you know can walk with me on the *Road to Recovery* and discover a new way of thinking and a path toward a new and better life.

All my best,
Cary John Efurd

Table of Contents

I Understand

If the name Jesus causes you to *cringe*, I understand. I felt the
same way. This book is about recovery, not religion—recovery
from drugs, alcohol, and mental illness. If you would like freedom
from worry, guilt, and shame, if regret, grief, and sorrow are more
than you can bear, this book is for you. If you have been battered,
shattered, and beaten up, I understand, because I've been there.
My life was all but crushed and destroyed, without hope.
The darkness of my life came from four DWIs, a reckless driving
account, arrest for disturbing the peace, arrest for public
drunkenness, and a restraining order placed on me by my ex-wife.
In 1977, I was diagnosed as manic-depressive with psychotic
features. Three times, I was admitted to mental wards of privately
funded hospitals. Two times, a state judge committed me to
Terrell State Hospital for the mentally ill. Alcohol helped me
endure the pain of my troubles. Rage and anger proved my points
on any subject.

There's more. I failed in business several times, filed for
bankruptcy, and killed a man while driving in a manic episode.
With estranged relationships and divorce, my children lived under
the roof of another man's house. I contemplated suicide and
hated to hear anyone talk about Jesus. His name made me cringe
with shame and guilt.

My whole life was built upon failures and disasters. The name
of Jesus made me fearful and apprehensive until the day I

discovered what that name could do for me. Now, he is alive and real in my life—bringing a peace that I had never dreamed was possible. My faith in God became a solid rock upon which I could stand.

In August 2004, my wife, Debby, and I began tithing as an act of faith. Since that time, we have experienced miracles that can't be explained apart from the reality of God working in our lives.

While continuing to tithe, we paid off our entire Chapter 7 bankruptcy. When our debtors would not or could not accept the money because the debt had been written off, we gave the exact amount to charity or to someone in need. We set up a trust fund for the young child of the man I killed. We began to give more than just the 10 percent.

We tithed on the gross amount of our income, not the net. Our first tithe was not in our budget. It was more than we could afford. I did not want to do it, because I couldn't see how that would be a benefit.

I was challenged by God's promise in the Bible. "Bring the whole tithe into the storehouse, that there may be food in my house. Test me in this," says the Lord Almighty, "and see if I will not throw open the floodgates of heaven and pour out so much blessing that there will not be room enough to store it" (Malachi 3:10).

God says we are stealing from him if we do not tithe. I say it like this: We have given away far more than we have, but we have far more than we ever dreamed. Since August 2004, we became successful in a business that materialized out of nowhere. God is why I am not dead already, and I'm not still a drunk who can't manage a mental illness. I haven't had a drink of alcohol in over thirty-five years. I take meds for the mental illness. It's like taking aspirin for a headache No big deal.

Now I understand how God heals lives. His covering sin works better than hiding in a bottle. Rejoice and be glad. God sent his Son for us to live victoriously here on Earth and in Heaven.

He can do that for you too.

Ditch Digging

With a can of roach spray nearby, I sat in my apartment to write a letter to my friend in Dallas. He had been my roommate, fraternity brother, and close friend at the University of Arkansas. I don't remember exactly what I wrote, but it was basically, *Hi, Ted. I just moved to Dallas.*

I went looking for work. I filled out one job application after another. Practicing rigorous honesty, which I had learned in AA, I had to disclose that I had just been released from Terrell State Hospital for the mentally ill. No job offers came.

The Texas Workforce Commission lobby was full of people looking for work, giving me little hope for finding a job on that day. I registered at the check-in desk and found a chair where I could sit and wait.

About thirty minutes later, a lady walked out and said, "Does anybody want to paint for $7.50 an hour?"

For that kind of money, I expected everybody to be waving their hands, begging to be chosen. I shot up from my chair and said, "Me! I'll work for $7.50 an hour. Standing there, hoping to be chosen, I looked around. I was the only person standing.

I got the job.

My car wasn't running, and I had no money to have it repaired. Each morning, I walked two blocks to the Dallas Transit bus stop, rode to the end of the line, and walked two miles to the jobsite. I didn't mind what it took to get there. I was happy that God had blessed me with a job.

I did such a good job at the new apartment complex that my boss gave me all the closets to paint. Pay day was every two weeks. After two weeks, I wasn't paid, but my boss asked me to stay on. After the third week, I still hadn't been paid. I trusted that he would, so I worked one more week. Never paid, I retired my paint brush.

God doesn't make a hole without filling it. On the same day that I quit work, I received a phone call at my apartment. We men living there had pooled a little money for a landline. The call was from Ted, my college roommate, who had received my letter. He invited me to his home for dinner with him and his wife. One of my friends at my apartment loaned me his car so I could go. The dinner was nice.

The next day, Ted phoned. He was a project manager for commercial construction sites all around Dallas. He told me where to go and who to meet on a jobsite. So I got on the bus and found the place. Praise God, I got a job was told I would start work on the following Monday.

I was thirty-three years old. By most standards, I should have been climbing the ladder to success, not looking for a bottom-rung job to get started. Many would have said I was a failure, but God always knows best. I needed to trust his standards, which were different.

I went to work.

God doesn't mess around, and I didn't think I should mess around either. Before going to work each morning, I spent a little time for devotions and prayer.

On one day in January 1987, during my devotional time, I had been working for seven months and copped an attitude. "God," I said, "I'm thirty-three years old, digging ditches, living in this little cockroach den with three men. What's next, already?"

Lo and behold, I looked down at the little black book I used for devotional reading, which said, *Be still and know that I am God.* Wow! Those words hit me like a dump truck load of dirt.

I have never forgotten that moment. I went to work with a new attitude. I asked myself, *How do I want to work for God?* The answer came: *Do the very best you can.* From that point on, I strived to be the very best ditch digger on the jobsite.

The superintendent became aware of my integrity and effort and called me into his office. "Efurd," he said, "you are an excellent worker. I have never seen a worker like you before. I want to send you to college, at company expense, so you can learn to read plans, operate instruments, and direct the setting of the concrete forms that you have been digging ditches for. And you will be getting a raise on your next paycheck."

Who but God could arrange a story like that?

Real Gain from Real Loss

In 2016, March winds came with much more than the roar of a lion. Gale-force winds over 90 mph uprooted trees and damaged roofs of hundreds of houses, including those managed by Efurd Maintenance LLC. Like every property manager I knew of, I was swamped with calls for repairs.

Storm-chaser vendors came into the area to capture works from all the property managers who needed help. The properties were owned by others. The catch phrase that said we were "renting 'em out and kicking 'em out worked well, because it was what owners liked to hear. We would take care of whatever they needed, so they didn't have to worry about anything. The saying was effective in lease presentations with tenants as a warning about what would happen for nonpayment of rent.

A storm-chaser vendor came by my office with all the required credentials, including proof of $1 million general liability insurance. I thought this was an answer to prayer.

God is real. I can't prove that with paper or a picture, but I can show you the evidence that becomes obvious when we obey him. My stronghold against God came tumbling down through obedience to giving tithes and offerings. Here was another case where I thought God was doing a miracle.

The storm chaser bid on the fence work at a house we managed in Grand Prairie, Texas, and needed $900 for material and supplies to get started. Since he was from out of town, that request sounded reasonable. He said the work would be finished in three days.

After three days, he hadn't come back for his payment for the work done. I phoned, but nobody answered. So I drove to the property and saw that no work had been done.

I said to myself, *My money is gone, and I won't be able to charge the owner for the $900. That's money out of my pocket. A total loss.* But then I remembered God's power and strength, saying, *God, that money is yours, no matter whether it's in my pocket or the storm chaser's. Bless the money, wherever it goes.* I immediately became settled in heart and mind.

From the time I began to tithe and give to his work, God had often revealed himself by blessing me in the face of losses. After I gave $500 to Hurricane Katrina in September 2005, I made $5,000 that I wasn't expecting. After I felt led quit my job and give up 100 percent of my income, God made his presence real to me with an opportunity to own 100 percent of a business. Feeling sure God would bless me again, I drove the eight miles back home, free from worry.

The moment I walked into my office, the phone rang. She was a stranger who found Efurd on the Internet. For a while, our conversation turned to God and his marvelous ways.

After a few minutes, she said, "You know, I'd like to do business with you, Cary. Can we meet on Tuesday at eleven o'clock?"

"Sure, I said. "Of course."

She arrived with an armload of nineteen file folders "Cary," she said, "my brother died in February and left me with these condominiums. I want you to manage them. They are fully occupied. The leases are up, and I want you to sell them. I will be giving all the proceeds to charity."

The portfolio of properties was worth $1.4 million. I don't know the exact percentage of increase on $900 stolen against the commission Efurd received for the management and sale of the properties. I just know the gain was a whole lot more than the loss.

When God is involved in our lives, we need not doubt when we offer praise to him by being obedient. He will make himself known to us, for Jesus lives in our praises. Obedience is the key that will open the door to proving our real he is.

Prayer Closet

In May of 2014, the real estate sales market began to improve. You could see the change like turning on a faucet, slowly at first. Then sales increased to a steady stream. Our property management business had been born from a depressed real estate sales market. In 2005–2006, as sellers were unable to sell their houses without taking heavy losses, Efurd Properties LLC (Efurd) began to help by leasing out their houses for monthly rental income. The revenue form leasing helped the owners make their note payments and moreover helped them keep their houses until the time of a better sales market.

Efurd's relationship with owners had been built over many years of service. When the sales market returned, we were the first in line to sell their houses—lots of houses. At its peak, Efurd managed about 550 houses (doors), including condominiums and duplexes.

Home sales for Efurd was good, but our primary business, property management, was stymied. New business for property management was not coming in. It's kind of hokey telling you this, but it's the truth of this story.

God is real, real in my life. It is true, I forget him, then I remember him, forget him, then I remember him. To help me remember him in my business, I went to Ben Franklin's Apothecary in Duncanville and purchased a bottle of baby oil. Efurd had just moved into its new office, the best office and location in Duncanville. Anybody in town would say the same. I determined that I would use the bottom drawer of my office desk as a place to keep the baby oil along with my Bible. I got an old piece of dusting cloth and put it in the drawer too. I decided that the baby oil would become "Holy Oil." I believe applying symbolism is an act of acknowledgement to the Most Holy One. It's no different than baptism being an outward sign of an inward decision. Baptism isn't what saves us, but we surely remember the dunking and the sprinkling.

In the evening of the day we moved into our new office, September of 2012, after everyone was gone for the day, I got out the holy oil and dust rag and squirted a little oil on the rag. I didn't wipe/soak everything down, but rather just walked behind the chairs of every employee, touched the cloth to the chairs and symbolically touched every doorway and surface area of desks and counters. I touched the entrance, the windows and walls, and the exit of the building. Then I walked around the building and went out as far as streets encompassing the building. I just said little prayers, how ever they came to my mind, and I was done. I changed the name of my personal office and for personal reasons identified it as my prayer closet. I didn't tell everybody. I just knew that it was and that I had consecrated my staff, my business, my building, customers and every passerby to God.

Now it is August of 2017. Efurd was 100 percent debt free. The home sales side of our business was being forced to keep property management afloat. I walked into my "prayer closet" and sat down in my chair. I was alone in my prayer closet and said out loud, "God, I am sixty-four years old. This business is taking a different path. If there is going to be an exit strategy, what's it going to be?" Thirty minutes later—I am pretty sure, *exactly* thirty minutes—I got a phone call from Century 21. The caller was my boss from the same property management company where I worked when it came to my mind that I should give up 100 percent of my income in obedience by quitting my job. I knew exactly what he wanted, before he even asked. He wanted to buy my company, but first he wanted to buy my lunch.

I told my old boss that we didn't need to go for lunch and to just come to my office. It happened just like this.

"Cary, I want to buy your company."

I showed him my books and asked him what it was worth to him. He told me, and in my belief, it was exactly the amount I had determined only days before.

We shook hands and Efurd was sold.

I don't know how to explain it happening. All I can tell about is "what happened." I do believe that when the time is right, it will happen for us all, no matter what the situation, good or bad. The symbolic ritual I performed did not sell the business for me. What it did for me is place God squarely in the middle of my business and my mind.

God is going to see us through. God has sovereign control over all things, good and bad.

Out of Control

On October 1, 1997, at the age of forty-four, twelve years without alcohol, eleven years discharged from Terrell State Hospital, nine years married to Debby, mental illness took control for the second major time in my life. And for the second time, it took away everything. It took away my business and my money. It stressed my family relationships, but this time it took another man's life.

After working for five years in commercial construction, I graduated in 1991 from North Lake College in Coppell, Texas, with a 4.0 GPA and Student of the Year status. I was married, not drinking, and feeling pretty good. I was in control.

Soon after graduation, I was laid off from my construction job due to a reduction in the workforce. Suddenly I had lost control. What was I going to do? Look for another job, of course. No, entrepreneurship had always been a way of life for me, so I went into business for myself.

I bought a portable carpet-cleaning machine from a friend in AA. My eleven-year-old daughter and I went up and down Horne street, where we lived, knocking on doors, looking for business. She came back with the first order for my new business, Sun Carpet Cleaning—a $50 carpet cleaning job.

The business grew into a full-fledged fire, smoke, and water damage restoration business, renamed Sun Cleaning and Restoration, LLC, with five full-time and up to eighteen part-time employees. We took professional classes to do our jobs well. I created a route to visit insurance companies at the same time every month, seeking business. And it worked. We kept growing.

Now, I was twelve years without alcohol, eleven years discharged from Terrell State Hospital, and nine years married to Debby. Success comes from being in control, and finally I had everything going my way.

But there was a problem.

In building the business, I purchased high-quality equipment, rented vehicles, and paid bills, even salaries, using my credit cards. I had accumulated so much debt that any bobble in monthly sales would put the business in jeopardy. Trying to grow the business too fast left me in a mess. I was stressed and strapped, unable to sleep for the worry.

I quit taking my bipolar medication. I told myself I didn't need it. I ignored what the doctors were saying. For hours on end, I stayed in my office, trying to figure out what to do next. Ultimately, the bipolar illness took over, leaving me out of control.

To escape the pressure, I needed to be alone—away from employees at work and my wife at home—so I took long drives. Sometimes I parked on the roadside and cried. I trembled in fear of what people would think. How could I pay my bills? I was sure to fail. While sitting in a Walmart parking lot, I screamed in desperation. I fingered God as my problem and cursed him aloud. Suicide came to mind. As goes the illness, with its ups and downs, highs and lows, I fell to the polar extreme of depression.

With no medication, poor sleep, little eating, and high stress, the illness quickly cycled through extreme highs and lows. It might be just a day, or it might be as little as an hour, my emotional and mental condition could change from high to low, then back to high and then dive to an even deeper low.

In the polar extreme of mania, when I thought conditions could get no worse, I crashed my blue Jeep into another Jeep and went airborne, landing with my passenger door pressed shut against the pavement. When I heard the explosion, I knew instinctively what had happened.

With the adrenaline and superhuman strength that came from the mania, I threw open the driver's door into the air and catapulted up and out to the pavement.

Someone said, "Help! Somebody help him."

The white Jeep was engulfed in flames.

I had no regard for my safety.

I ran to the Jeep to see the man's clothes burn away. As I watched his seat belt burn, the flames parted as God seemed to be waiting for his moment to show up.

I reached in. "Let's go, buddy. Let's get you out of here."

He reached toward me and clasped his big hands onto my forearms. As I pulled him out with great force, I felt his skin peeling and slipping away. The skin on my hands was burning too.

With the same energy as before, I picked him up in my arms and carried him away from the roaring flames that had now fully engulfed his Jeep. I stood him up, trembling and praying that he would be all right.

A crowd was gathering from the apartment complex. Someone said he needed to lie down.

As I knelt beside the man, I said to the crowd, "Everybody pray. Please! Everybody just pray." Then I said, "God, come here. Please!"

The man's name was Gabriel, eighteen years old, 6' 2" tall and a muscular 245 pounds. He had a young wife and an eight-month-old baby boy.

"Tell my wife that I love her," Gabriel said.

"No," I said. "You are going to tell her yourself."

With the last effort of a dying man, he reached out, grabbed my collar, and pulled me toward him. "Promise me that you will tell my wife that I love her."

"I will," I said. "Yes, I will."

The next day, on October 2, 1997, at 3:00 p.m., Gabriel died.

Gabriel could not have known I was the man who caused the accident that killed him. He knew me only as the man who pulled him out of the fire and would give his dying words of love to his wife.

The only thing that did not burn in the fire was the Gabriel's Bible. Had the flames parted to save the Bible? The burning of Gabriel's hands left scars caused by his fingers pressing into my forearms. When I look at the scars today, I think, *These are Gabriel's fingerprints.*

Because of Gabriel, my life has changed forever. It continues to change. With his death, while tragic, he will have an eternal reward in Heaven for how he died for me. Gabriel was a victim of my mental illness. His death brought a revelation that compelled me to recover as wholly as possible from mental illness so I could help others.

If you have a mental illness, listen to me with your heart, mind, and soul. Do not let your illness go untreated. Mental illness will take you down along with others around you. Things have happened to all of us that we can look at and say, "God brought this out of that, good out of bad." In AA, it's said, "We do not regret the past, nor wish to shut the door on it. We see how our experience, strength, and hope can help another human being."

Using our experiences as a foundation for building a better life, our regrets will subside, and others will be helped.
."

Scared

Mother was playing the piano, and Neal Ray was leading the songs while I panicked in the pew at Crossroads Missionary Baptist Church during a two-week revival. The young preacher was just out of seminary, getting his chance to practice his calling. He wasn't much over twenty years old, and I was twelve.

I didn't want to be in church. I hated the songs at the end of the services: "Just as I Am" for the day services and "Oh Why Not Tonight?" for the evening services. At the end of each service, the time came when people asked to come forward, repent, and be saved. This was called "walking the aisle." Others called it "the altar call." I called it "terrible" because of the way it made me feel.

Part of me wanted to walk the aisle because of what I knew it would mean for my parents. I somehow thought it might relieve the pain I felt. But I resisted. I knew I was supposed to go because everybody told me I should. On the last day of the revival, I had stood firm through the last song.

I never moved.

I was at the vestibule doorway, headed for outside when two hands grabbed my shoulders, stopped me.

The young preacher turned me around and looked me straight in the eye. "Don't you want to be saved?"

I mumbled something. I don't remember exactly what, because I didn't have a good answer.

With one hand on my shoulder, he led me down the aisle to the front row while others were leaving. If I had refused to go and flopped down on the floor, I think he would have dragged me down the aisle, with me kicking and screaming. Soon, he and I were the only ones left in the country church.

Again the preacher looked me in the eye. "Do you want to be saved?"

At twelve years old, I knew the answer he wanted, but the feeling I had was indescribable. Was it stress? Fear? Simply stated, I was scared.

"If you want to be saved," he said, "put your hand in mine. Close your eyes, and pray after me."

I did what he said, repeating every word, and then headed for the door with a pat and a push from the young preacher's hand at my back.

For many years, I questioned whether I was really saved. But if repeating a prayer is all it takes to be saved, then I was destined for Heaven on that August day in 1966—Saturday the thirteenth. I was baptized the next day, on Sunday, in Neal Ray's pond.

It's said that one never forgets the moment of one's salvation, and I have never forgotten the year, month, day, and the moment when I said yes to the Lord.

Two years later, I had my first drunk.

.

God Is Real

By 2007 our real estate company had outgrown the space we rented at the Keller Williams real estate location on Mockingbird Lane in Dallas, Texas. I had worked enough time under the licensing of another broker to become my own broker. I applied and took the Texas brokers exam. I passed the test.

Efurd Properties LLC had been established since 2005. We were managing over 200 properties by then. We had a staff of three full-time employees, including myself and one showing agent, who brought in rental applications. Add Debby, who worked a full-time job in addition to working in the business full-time.

Debby is an amazing wife, confidante, business partner, lover, and friend. She's got a lot of tenacity and business sense.

Efurd Properties would not have been so successful had it not been for God's intervention through Debby's life. Debby keeps me straight. She is my helpmate.

Debby found a nice office building in Duncanville, where we lived. We signed a five-year lease, remodeled to suit our needs, and moved in. I was twenty-two-years sober by then, fifty-three years old (it's never too late by The Way to start over. He is The Way).

We had been tithing and giving above and beyond the tithe since 2004. In 2006, God had given me the challenge to give back that $5,000 I've told you about. I met the challenge. When the challenge presented itself, I wanted to back away from it. *God, $5,000 is a lot of money,* I'd say. *I really don't have it.* I had to give it, because I wanted to keep it so bad. I had asked God on the day someone gave me the $5,000, *God, how will I ever be able to give $5,000 to someone in need?* One of the greatest gifts I have ever received was the emotional relief of tears, joy, and gratitude by the receiver of the $5,000. She needed the money as bad or worse than I had, back in 2005. It happened exactly one year to the month, probably the exact day, that the same $5,000 had been given to me in Salt Lake City, Utah.

I had begun listening to God in a new way. The old way was to read his Word, hear his Word, and then *not* do his Word. Tithing is how I have come to deepen my faith and know that God is real. There are other ways to know God is real. They all center around obedience. Money, the power and love of money, had always been my stronghold against God. The old standard from Crossroads Missionary Baptist Church, "My God is real . . . deep in my soul," comes to mind. For me, to prove God is real is Cary John Efurd trying to obey him and take him at his word."

By the time we sold our business in August of 2017, our team, but my name as the Broker/Realtor, was ten years running ranked in the top 100 of over 8,000 agents in the DFW Metroplex.

Trust and obey. There is no other Way to be happy in Jesus. Seek professional help if you need it. I've had a lot of professional help. God is not compartmentalized to just a church. He came to me on a mental ward at Terrell State.

Mother's Love

On November 18th, 2019, my mother, Sandra Martin Efurd, died at Southern Winds Manor in Pittsburg, Texas. She raised four boys. In order, they were named Cary John, Richard Kent, Steven Michael, and Gregory Martin. We were all there for Mother's passing moments. Alongside were other family members, friends, hospice, staff of SWM, her brother Jimmie Kent Martin, Johnny "Big Man" Smith, Deborah Jan (my wife), Lauren Efurd Lowrey, her brother Tyler Efurd, and God.

I don't know how she pulled it off, but that love knows no bounds. Today, you could ask any one of us boys which of us was mother's favorite son. We'd all raise our hands at the same time and say in unison, "I was." Not a one of us would dispute the other. We were all her favorite son. What a day that will be when my mother I will see.

Mother carried her love for me from my cradle to her grave. There will never be another woman like her.

Like Papaw, she loved unconditionally, but had great expectations for her children. She cleaned us, dressed us, fed us, carried us with her when she went places, and made sure we had a corsage for our dates (I always asked for orchids). She made sure I had straight teeth and taught me to smile by example of her own smile. In later life, she and Daddy (John Hart Efurd) drove me to college. They then came back to get me and my wrecked Volkswagen, due to my first DWI during my second semester in college (University of Arkansas). Papaw bought me another Volkswagen to drive back.

How much trust and forgiveness can a parent give? I believe it is as much as God has to offer parents. The shame and disappointment of failure in my life was taking hold of me in a big way at that point. I didn't wreck any more cars while in college, but I did have three more DWIs. I did not make it through college for a degree. I went on to achieve academic expulsion with a .70 GPA. Thank goodness for golf and bowling, right?

When I came home, the shame of defeat in my life, carried out by my own hand, warred against the expectations and love of Papaw, Mamaw, Mother, and Dad. Let me say it like this: I was in a living hell of shame and defeat. I went into my time-honed default method of covering up my guilt feelings and drank more alcohol.

The family didn't give up on me. For a short time, I went to the orchards and helped Dad prune peach trees (Dad and Mother were the establishing duo and originators of Efurd Orchards). No one in the family ever came to me and said I was a lost cause. Instead, I believe, out of concern and worry, they tried always to help. How much help can one person need? My answer now is the question: How many times will God forgive us?

It was tough love, the best kind of love that finally came out in my parents. My mother and dad committed me for a journey back home into Terrell State Hospital, thirty-six years ago.

Glory be to God Almighty. Amen.

Thanks

I had no idea what would happen when I posted my story yesterday. But I know that God's plan for me is for good, and you too, you know. There have been many positive replies and many positive reactions. I believe that many who read the testimony have also shared it with friends and family members. You have the "goods" on me now.

Truth never hurts. Truth sets us free. Your trust in him, God, brings us through every trial, every doubt, every fear. Give way to the Truth, the whole Truth and nothing but the Truth, and we are set free.

There is nothing wrong with any of us but denying that we aren't perfect. We want to be perfect. We sometimes think we are perfect, but the freedom found in Truth says we are not perfect, never will be, subject closed. It's such a good truth to accept. Hallelujah! Amen.

The help we find in Jesus, I believe, is for all people, without prejudice. We must obey to let God do the judging on Judgment Day. Will we ever be perfect? Absolutely, one day yonder. I'm pretty sure there is an old hymn I used to sing at Crossroads Missionary Baptist Church: "One glad morning when this life is over . . ."

Thank you for your response to the post yesterday. This is an all in one thanks to all of you and to the King of Kings. He has the whole world in His hands.

Hound Dog

It was about May of 2005. Debby and I had been tithing since the August before, in 2004. We had stepped it up a bit by giving over and above. I was liking the way things were going. Increase was coming.

The way I understand Malachi 3:10 was just the way it read, He said, "You can prove me in this. Give the first fruits of your income and see if I won't open the windows of heaven and pour down blessings you can't hold" (paraphrased). I was keeping up with the percentages of the return.

Now keeping up with percentages may not really be the way it should be done, but it is a way of "counting blessings." When I was keeping up with percentages, I found that the Lord returned in exacts: 100 percent, 10 percent, etc. The story I'm about to tell you had to do with a 42 percent increase of my paycheck in one fell swoop. God works in mysterious and miraculous ways. You probably know that and may have heard it since a very young age.

I was sitting in my office one day in, I think, May of 2005. My boss stopped by and said to me, "Cary, I want you to do this." He then described what it was he wanted me to do.

I was working for a large property management company. We covered about every county connecting Dallas County. The property management company was part of the larger real estate company that owned twenty-eight offices across the Metroplex. The real estate market in Dallas at the time was suffering low volume sales, and prices were tanking. Houses were not selling. Prices were low. What we, the property management, could do to help the sellers was to take the houses under our management, rent them out, and hold them until the sales market came back.

What my boss did (I say, God did) was give me every single lead that came in from hundreds of realtors across the area. God made me in that moment "the man" on the property management scene. My first check was 42 percent more than the last I'd gotten.

To him who is given much, much is required. I learned the lesson like this: I was happy and going and giving God all the praise, and counting, when it happened. It came as a surreal moment, in the twinkling of an eye. I had just returned from the Lions Club and sat down in my chair when something came over me. In that moment I knew that I must give up 100 percent of my income. I knew that I must quit my job. Anything less would be a lack of faith. I could have given my checks each week indefinitely, but I believed God wanted more of my faith. In the same twinkling of the eye, I got up, went to my boss and told him I would be resigning my position.

He asked why.

I told this God-fearing, tithing boss man that I believed God wanted me to.

I did stay on until he found someone to take my place.

To fill in some of the story, in 2004 I was elected to be the president of the Greater Dallas Chapter of the National Association of Residential Property Managers. I fervently worked at the position. Our chapter garnered many accolades across the nation in the NARPM community. People were talking about our growth. The national president called me out of the blue one day and invited me to California to meet with other presidents and the NARPM board members. While there, I was asked to be the emcee of the coming national convention in Salt Lake City, Utah, to be held in September.

God was working on something. I didn't know what. He's still working on something and I still don't know what. But it would then and will now all turn out right and good. I had given back to God 100 percent of my income.

A replacement had been found at my work. I had no income. I was headed to Salt Lake City to be emcee of the national convention for NARPM. Hurricane Katrina had just hit in August. I was a little nervous. People were telling me what to do.

The room was packed with seasoned property managers, looking at me up there, waiting for me to do something. I pulled out my old standby and gave 'em a real rendition of "Hound Dog," by Elvis Presley. It worked. The crowd began clapping with the song and cheering when it was over. I've been singing "Hound Dog" since Cecil Guest would pay me a nickel to do it, when I was seven or eight. I no longer do it for money. I do it by request only, but sometimes I just stand up and do it. I'm told I sound like Elvis. I guess I do. That's what they say.

After the song and a little welcoming of the crowd, it came to my mind that an offering should be taken to send to Katrina victims. It came to mind too that I should start the offering with a $500 donation. What happened then was that we collected over $68,000 dollars for Katrina victims.

I didn't have $500. I called Debby and asked her to wire the money.

Now, I told you about the National recognition of our Dallas chapter. We really raked in the plaques for various members. I was recipient of the President's Award, and the glory goes to God.

Then, a remarkable thing happened. A person came to me and said, "I want you to be the publicist for the California State Convention of NARPM. Here is $5,000. I'm paying you in advance." Go figure. Who is God? Not me.

My very next thought was, *God, how will I ever be able to give $5,000 to someone who needs it?* I've since had my chance and seized it. Glory be to God on High.

I used the $5,000 to start my own property management company, Debby and me. Amen.

Patience

We have patience when the Holy Spirit works through us. The Holy Spirit is God personified in Jesus, his Son. Except by Jesus, no one can know God or have the presence of the Holy Spirit, the very Spirit of God, which includes patience.

Job in the Bible is an example of a patient man. He lost his possessions, children, and the support of his wife. You might say, "Job lost it all." Still, Job trusted God.

Moses, by faith, led a nation through a parted sea and trials for forty years, into God's Promised Land.

We, you and I, have traveled through many hardships in our years on Earth. We have lost, rebelled, complained, worried, and feared about the future. But what has happened? Some of us have come to faith in God through Jesus Christ. By the examples of faith, we have seen in people like Job, Moses, our parents, friends, and so many before us, we have taken up our crosses (troubles), given them to Jesus, and made easy the load we carry.

It's true. We are on a journey of faith. It is a daily, moment-by-moment journey. The joy we find by our trust in God has been made real on Earth as it is in Heaven. Through the life and example of Jesus, God in Heaven came down to us here on Earth.

May we trust you more, O God. Lead us easily through our troubles. We accept the kind patience you have given us. Give us a long fuse in patience until the coming of your Son, Jesus, in whose name we pray exceedingly for the lost yet to come to salvation. Thank you. Amen.

Doing What's Right

My grandfather taught me not to borrow anything from anyone. The Bible warns of the dangers of debt and wisdom says that it is best not to accumulate debt. I've done both. I have borrowed cars, implements and money. Proverbs 22:7 says, "The rich rules over the poor, and the borrower is the slave of the lender." It is said that debt is a form of slavery. I can testify that it is true. The Bible teaches that if we borrow, we are to pay back what we borrowed. The payback usually comes with a form of interest attached.

I borrowed so much money in a business that I owned in Dallas County, Texas, that I was forced to file bankruptcy. Everything surrounding the bankruptcy had to do with the trouble I was having with mental illness, a tragic accident that took a life, and lack of cash flow because I was not able to go out and sell services. The slavery of debt helped induce me through worry into a mental state that had potential to destroy. Thus, it was my doing in the accumulation of debt by not taking care of my illness and by not seeking and following sound advice.

Growing up, I would hear grownups say, "That man filed bankruptcy." People saying such, with the tone they said it, left me with the perception and belief that anyone filing for bankruptcy was a bad person.

When I faced bankruptcy, I found myself thinking that I was bad, which added to the despair I felt.

30

I no longer believe that people who file bankruptcy are bad, but I do believe that the Bible teaches that anyone who takes on debt should plan to repay it. When I filed bankruptcy in 1998, I sought Christian counseling to help direct me. It was after the accident and I was in a recovery of trying to quiet a desperate mental state. Debby was by my side.

The Christian counselor was named Larry Burkett, who founded Crown Financial Ministries. Larry died in 2003 at the age of 64. Larry said, "It is okay to file for bankruptcy, but rightfully you owe the money and should pay it back." It stung a little bit to hear those words, but I knew he was right. I committed in my heart to pay the money back.

Before the payback came this: I went through a period of praying and lamenting over the situation of a bankrupt business, the future of my employees, and a deep depression over the young man dying in the accident I had caused. I grouped all of this in a big pot and stirred and stirred it in my mind, heart, and soul until I heard the words of Debby, saying, "Cary, don't let that boy's life go in vain." Her words are still clear in my mind today.

In the nighttime of that day in February 1998, a moment of clarity came to me. I realized that, in my heart, I did not intend to kill that young man. I became clean in an instant. Regarding the business and employees, I got up the next morning and said to Debby, "I am going to the office and close down the business."

I arrived at the office at straight up 6:00 a.m. I know because when I put the key in the door and turned, the phone inside rang, as though it were on cue with the doorknob turning. I looked at my watch, and it was six o'clock straight up. I wondered, *Who in the world is calling at this time of morning?* I stepped into my office and answered the phone.

It was David, someone I knew through AA. I didn't know him well, but I did know him well enough. The first words out of his mouth were, "Cary, what are you doing?"

I said to him, "David, I am here to shut down my business."

David said, "Don't do it. I'll buy it from you."

David paid me enough in cash to pay my employees' salaries for two weeks. He took over the lease of the building as well as the leases we had on certain restoration equipment. He also kept my staff on payroll. My staff still had a job. God was on time—his time.

Turns out that during one of the lowest circumstances of my life, when all seemed lost, all I had to do was get up and go. Get up and take action. I don't even think that I believed real hard that everything would be okay. I just prayed, lamented, and listened to the words of Debby. "Cary, don't let that boy's life go in vain." There are spiritual advisors in our lives, and sometimes they are as close as a brother, a sister, a friend, or a spouse.

Debby and I paid back the bankruptcy debt. It only took a few years of easy payments and doubling up when we could. When we'd go to a bank, for instance, who would not take a payment because they had already written off the debt, we'd give the same amount to a charity or church, or to someone in need. I just wanted what was not mine to be out of my pockets, just as fast as I could get it out.

I am still learning this lesson. If I will do what is right in every circumstance, every circumstance will work out. I don't believe we even need faith to do what is right.

Obedience does not need faith to work. Faith comes by practicing obedience. Trust comes when we see the practice of obedience work in our lives. Obedience delivers results by its own nature. The true nature of God is found in obedience. Trust and obey, for there is no other way to be happy in Jesus but to trust and obey.

God loves us. We have God's instructions in written form.

Never Give Up

In construction, sometimes the economy forces a slowdown. In one of these times, before I was married to Debby and while living in a state-funded mental health transition apartment with three other men, I found myself out of work. Because I had been employed for several months, the State of Texas had ended the $50.00 per week subsidy that I had used to pay for essentials.

In AA there is what is called Tradition 7, which says "Every AA group ought to be self-supporting, declining outside contributions." I personalized Tradition 7 of Alcoholics Anonymous by committing to refuse outside contributions, which included the state subsidy, were it to be offered to me again. As God would have it, my mother, my daddy, and my grandmother all called me at different times on the same day, with them not knowing that others had called. Each of them offered me money. I could not take the money, because of the commitment that, going forward, I would not take money from anyone again. Hadn't they already given enough? And wasn't my God bigger than not having a job?

I must tell you that I am not as much of a spiritual giant as it may sound. I would like to be, but I am not. During my time in Terrell, my mother and daddy had taken on my obligation to distribute the *Dallas Morning News* in Camp County, Pittsburg, Texas, every morning, seven days a week, starting at 4:00 a.m. This meant they got up every morning by 3:30 to be there in time for the delivery truck for the paper and to see to it that the newspapers were banded and bagged in people's yards and driveways, on time—hail, sleet, rain, snow, or hot. They did it. They used the money to pay for the child support I owed each month. They did it for seven years and never muttered a complaint. My mother and daddy were the spiritual giants! I can only hope to be the kind of people they were.

Having said that, what I did next was easy. I determined that I would go out and not come back until I found a job. I walked north up Davis Street in Oak Cliff, Texas, until I ran out of businesses to ask for work and then started back south, stopping everywhere to ask for a job. It happened just like this: I went into The Pit Grill on the corner of Davis and Hampton, and not unlike years later, asking for a property management job with Keller Williams Realty on Mockingbird Lane, I said to the manager, "I am looking for a job as a fry cook."

He said, "Well, we are looking for a fry cook. When can you start?"

I said, "Now!"

He handed me a white apron and showed me to the flat grill where I started frying eggs, bacon, sausage, and everything else that was on the menu—waffles, hamburgers, grilled cheese sandwiches, add it all. My experience as owner and operator of C.J.'s Barbecue was now paying off in spades.

How does God answer our commitments to doing the right thing? He answers by supplying all of our needs. I was now making $5.25 per hour, earned free meals just for working at The Pitt Grill.

I was two blocks from where I lived. I walked to work, saving money on gas. I worked the evening shift, so when my construction job called me back a few weeks later, I had two jobs—two jobs, and I was able to make $600.00 per week. That was pretty good money back in 1986.

I have learned the lesson, time and time again, that lamenting with worry never helps. The Bible says, do not worry. It is a command, and the Bible says it like this in Matthew 6:25–26:

"Therefore I tell you, do not worry about your life, what you will eat or drink; or about your body, what you will wear. Is not life more than food, and the body more than clothes? Look at the birds of the air; they do not sow or reap or store away in barns, and yet your heavenly Father feeds them. Are you not much more valuable than they?"

How powerful is that? It is more powerful than a locomotive and able to leap tall challenges in a single acceptance of Truth.

We are not to be irresponsible and sit back. We must go out determined to find what God has in store for us. It is always for our good. He has set his plans that we should prosper and find peace. Remember, "do not worry" is a command, the same as going out to seek the good he has for us.

Everything is a decision for obedience. When we fail, and we will, the command is to call on him and seek him with our prayers.

One of the comments I received today, reminded me, "God does not always meet our expectations, but he will surely exceed them." Two of the tools to find God's will are patience and long-suffering. In other words, never give up.

Borrowing

One of the primary reasons I began writing these posts to be included in a coming book, *To L and Back*, is so that my family may know me for something other than mental illness, craziness, and insanity. I am hopeful that the insanities of my life will be seen as cured by a deep and abiding faith, showing that the love of God does overwhelmingly overcome the destruction of alcoholism, mental illness, and failures—in relationships, business, and otherwise.

In 2002, I had my first game of catch in the back yard with my son, who was twenty-six years old at the time. I celebrated his birthday by hiding treasure-hunt notes with clues around the yard and in the house. One clue led him to find the next clue. Ultimately, the final clue led him to turn on a ceiling fan in the living room where twenty-dollar bills had been placed on top of the blades. When my son turned on the fan, the bills scattered upward and then floated down. It was fun. I love my son. He is one of the finest men I know.

He and I talk about one of the few things I taught him in his growing-up years, and that was to whistle real loud—real loud, ear-piercing loud. It was not the pucker-and-blow kind of whistle. It is the other kind of whistling without using fingers. I can still see him in the carpet-cleaning van as we were driving to and from jobs. He'd hunker down in the passenger's seat and blow and blow. Then it happened after about four hours of trying. He sounded out his first whistle. We were both elated and laughing over the accomplishment. Pretty soon, he was whistling as loud as I could. Later, and even now, when we want the other's attention, we whistle. Our whistles come in handy. Once when we were lost from each other in a crowd at a football game in Dallas, we whistled for each other. I know his whistle, and he knows mine. By a whistle we were no longer lost from each other.

God brings restoration to tragedy. I did not choose to be bipolar. It chose me. I did not choose my children. God gave them to me. There is a lot that I did choose, though. Today, I choose to believe that God has enabled me to become a better person and make better choices to help God in the restoration process of my family. "I am available" is primarily what I believe my grown children know about me today.

If you think that God does not care about the little things and all things concerning your life, listen to his Holy Voice, the Holy Spirit of his love inside of you. Capture your mind's thoughts and submit them to God. Make them as pure as the driven snow by supplication and meditation. You will fail to listen to him over and again, but he does not fail to come when you call. Cry out to him as often as it takes. He knows your voice. Make your voice your whistle to the Father, who loves you, and you don't have to feel lost any longer.

I remind you that I have had a lot of professional help. God came to me and healed me through the care of Terrell State Hospital and professional counselors. Be not ashamed of anything. See how your experience, strength, and hope can help another human being. God enables us with power and makes us bold to speak for his glory.

In April of 2020, a friend called me on the phone just to catch up. We hadn't talked in a while. I was on the back porch smoking cigarettes, drinking tea, and taking a break from doing nothing. But I was considering whether or not to buy or rent a tiller to pull behind my tractor so I could repair feral hog damage in my hay meadow. I mentioned my considerations to my friend.

He said, "Cary John, go over to my house and get my tiller. It's already hooked up. Use my tractor too."

I said, "No, I do not like to borrow."

Well, my friend insisted.

I said, "I'll borrow your tiller, but I'd like to use my John Deere tractor."

My friend met me at his house, and together we disconnected his tiller and hooked it to my tractor. I drove off heading to till my meadow.

I live on the farm, in the very house where I grew up with my three younger brothers. Down in the area where I wanted to begin tilling was a gully that had been created over the years by the watershed off the sloping grade of the banks on either side. When I was growing up, Daddy used trash, briars, bushes, and small trees. One of the first things I did when Debby and I moved to Pittsburg was clean out, clean up, and burn off the ravine where much debris had been discarded over the years and left to be grown over by the weeds, trees, grass, briars, and plants. One of the many things in the ravine were twenty-five to thirty big, thick rubbery items. The best way I can describe them is to tell you that these items were not unlike the kind of thick rubber that is found on truck docks, attached for the trailer trucks to back up to and be stopped short of damage to truck and trailer. These rubbery things I am telling you about may have been the discard from the molds used to form these dock pads. They were large, thick and heavy, with cut-outs leaving square and rectangular holes from a molding machine.

Within five minutes of operation of the tilling machine, I ran across a piece of the thick rubber and tangled and lodged it in the borrowed tiller. The tiller was damaged beyond repair.

I immediately remembered what my grandfather had taught me. In his words, "Don't borrow anything from anybody."

38

First Year in College

I was fighting forces much bigger than myself, and they were battles that I did not know how to fight. I had gone through adolescence, graduated from high school, and found myself in college. It was spring of 1972. To add to the already painful urges I had for alcohol, I became involved with drugs and mixed them with alcohol.

My college life was a failure in the sense that most people go to college for an education and a degree. I guess I had the same illusion in mind, but what I came away with were failing grades, four DWIs, a reckless driving violation, a disturbing the peace conviction, and a night in jail as a public drunk. My college career ended with a mandatory academic expulsion with a cumulative GPA of .70. The failure added to the shame and guilt that had come to burden me every single moment of my life.

I had a job in college. I was a bartender at the Fayetteville Country Club. I drank at will. I'd slip outside and take a toke off a joint that I'd hide in one of the side pockets of the bartender's vest. I met a lot of very important and rich people at the country club. The bartending job gave me a little bit of self-worth, I guess. The one important person that impressed me was a Budweiser beer distributor. He gave me tip money.

My first DWI coincided with the popular campus-wide spring party hosted by the fraternity to which I belonged. It was called Catfish Row. I had begun drinking early in the day of the event, a

Saturday, and was feeling no pain when I picked up my date late in the afternoon. My date lived on campus, less than a quarter of a mile away. She and I made it to the party and, I guess, had a good time. I don't remember. One of my friends offered to drive my date home. Being drunk with alcohol and bursting with obstinate rebut, I would not hear of it. I managed (thank God) to get her safely to the parking lot of the student housing where she lived. My date asked me repeatedly if she could drive me back, her telling me that I could pick my car up the next day. I told her that I was fine and somehow negotiated the car out of the parking lot.

The cars on the street where my frat house was located, were parked and lined on both sides of the narrow street: Stadium Drive in Fayetteville, Arkansas, where Razorback Stadium was located. At the point of being almost in front of my destination, I apparently blacked out, passed out, lost consciousness (however you want to say it). The next thing I remember seeing was the blue lights swirling on top of the two campus security cars that had arrived on the scene. I saw the best friend I had, run down the slope of the front yard of the frat house. He asked me if I was okay.

In a drunken stupor, I said yes.

As my best friend and in fraternal posture, he said that he would tell the police that he was driving. His offer was with good intention until he saw that his car was one of the six cars that I had hit. I had hit one car and then scraped down the sides of 5 other parked cars. I was driving a red Volkswagen that Papaw had bought for me.

The motor, being in the rear, was not damaged and allowed for the car to still crank. I remember vividly asking the police to let me go. I cranked the car and reached for the gear shift, as the officer said, "You are not going anywhere."

He was right. I could not find the stick shift of the Volkswagen in the place where it was supposed to be. The stick

40

had broken off in the crash and was lying in the passenger side floorboard.

"Please, God, please."

One of my cell mates pulled a knife from his pocket and put it to my throat and told me to stop crying. I dried up the crying the best I could and sat down on the concrete bench, which was also used for sleeping. I laid back. The event sobered me and I sank into depression and fear as I began to realize that my mother and daddy were going to find out what had happened. My first year in college wasn't going very well at all.

Gift that Keeps on Giving

I see now that one of the biggest gifts of love that my mother and dad ever gave me was having the irrevocable commitment papers drawn up by a state judge, which sent me to Terrell State Hospital on New Year's Eve of 1984. Like an animal trapped and raging in a cage, I was confined with no way out.

Anger consumed me. I'd rage in thoughts to myself and scream aloud the thoughts that were fashionable to bipolar anger: "I don't belong in here! You are the crazy people! Let me out!" There were always plenty of blanks filled in with expletives included.

The tirades of shouting in anger always ended with me wrestling and fighting three male nurses. The male nurses always won and would force me back into a secluded padded cell and give me more shots of Thorazine.

Going through treatment at TSH forced me to focus on a mental illness with which I was diagnosed in 1977 by the late Dr. Baskins in Tyler, Texas. Before TSH, I had been treated by various doctors in three private mental wards in Tyler. These stays were short one- to three-week stays. I went along with being checked in at the hospitals, I guess because the illness had not yet grown into complete defiance of everybody and everything in my life. I was married, had children and a business during these short stays in the private hospital mental wards.

Short visits in treatment weren't enough for me to find a way of recovery. God bless the men and women counselors and doctors who tried, but I could not then see why I was there, except to appease my mother and daddy, my wife, and my unsuspecting children. All I wanted was to get along, get out, and go back to my business, and then be along my merry way, which included drinking alcohol that purged the bipolar medication out of my system.

Terrell State Hospital saved my life, and Alcoholics Anonymous consummated the salvation. God saved my soul from Hell. TSH and AA saved me from me. Mother and Dad gave me a gift that keeps on giving.

Thank you, John Hart and Sandra, for loving me enough to do what you may have thought to be the unthinkable. Amen.

Sam and Helen

In January of 1987, I moved out of the state-funded apartment where I had been living since being discharged from TSH and into an apartment with a woman I had met in AA. Our relationship was doomed from the beginning, though I could not see it at the time. The relationship lasted for five months.

For me, the difficulty in being a Christian is because I have my old self to contend with. It keeps cropping up and seems to catch me unawares. It is no easy battle for me to completely and successfully resist temptation. Living with the woman as I did was a lesson learned about myself and the mistake of promiscuity.

I met Sam E, a substance abuse counselor at TSH, while I was sitting on a piano bench strumming my guitar. I was living on "L" ward. Sam walked over and sat down on the piano bench beside me. He began to talk. Sam gave me an introduction to Alcoholics Anonymous by asking me if I wanted to go to an AA meeting in Rockwall, Texas.

Sam drove me and three other men to the AA meetings in his car named "White Lightning." At first, meetings were an opportunity for me to get off the ward, but going to the meetings with Sam helped begin a pattern of recovery that led to the tens of thousands of meetings I have attended since. My first meeting was in January of 1985, eight months before I had my last drink.

The first AA meeting didn't prevent me from having my last drink, but it did help me to have one last drink on September 13,

1985, while home for a weekend pass. More fuel I had added to Mother and Dad's worry. It was unknown to them that by that one last drink I had begun making a living amends to them by staying sober. Saying the words, "I'm sorry," was no longer enough. Being taken back to the hospital in a drunken state was a complete embarrassment.

I had finally hit bottom, as if a commitment and a strait jacket were not enough. Continuing with meetings in Rockwall, I said to Sam, "Sam, I am never going to take another drink." I meant it and I haven't. Mother and Dad died many years later, knowing I was living without alcohol.

To be successful in AA, I believe it is imperative for recovery to have a sponsor. I see it now that it was part of Sam's job as a substance-abuse counselor to act in a temporary sponsorship roll to those who went with him to the meetings. I learned from Sam that he was in recovery and had a sobriety date. At the time I met Sam, he was eleven years sober, and his sobriety date was August 27th, the same date as my "navel" birthday, as it's called in AA. Sam was the only sponsor I ever had. He died sober in 2019, with forty-five years of sobriety. We attended a meeting together only a few months before he passed away, and we spoke often on the phone over the many years.

It is not probable and highly unlikely, and I imagine, not condoned by an employer, that a counselor of a mental hospital would take sponsorship of a patient from a mental hospital after discharge, and certainly should not invite one of the "crazies" into their home. As God would have it, Sam became my sponsor and invited me into his home in Dallas, Texas.

Having settled into my new home, the roach-infested apartment, I found myself eating home cooking by Helen and swimming in Sam and Helen's backyard pool. I went with Sam to AA meetings at the Aquarius Group on Lovers Lane. I got my first-, second-, and third-year sobriety chips at Aquarius.

With no place to go after moving out of the apartment where I lived with the woman, I called Sam. He had me come by his house. After discussing the matter with Helen, he agreed that I could stay in their home for three days.

Sam said, "After three days, you will have to go." Sam was a kind and considerate man who believed in helping, but believed moreover that "people need to make their own way by their own merit."

I called the state-funded program and was able to secure a different apartment in Oak Cliff, where I lived with two other men. The apartment was roach-free and had a huge swimming pool right outside my door.

Thank you, Sam and Helen, for all you did for me and for being a living sponsor by example to hundreds upon hundreds of other men and women of Alcoholics Anonymous.

No matter how far down the scale I have gone, I only pray that my experience can benefit others. Amen.

Self or God

These posts are not intended to absolve myself of my wrongdoings, nor to elevate myself to sainthood. Only God through the saving grace of his son Jesus Christ can do either.

It is the same for all believers in the faith of Jesus Christ. Unbelief is what condemns us, makes us miserable. I believe all believers can have unbelief, even in salvation. I believe the kind of unbelief experienced by believers is better identified as doubt.

Doubt is a separation (the believer from God) and causes depression, anger, pride, jealousy, hate, laziness, and greed to take root. All of these wrongs can flourish if not addressed by the regeneration of faith by seeking God's will in our hearts and minds.

My writings will not allow me to exhaustively pursue a complete exposition of what the Bible says about any given topic written herein. I am not a Bible scholar. I have no formal training and no degree in biblical studies. What I know, I learned in Sunday school, listening to sermons and by Bible study through the years of my life.

I do not expect that all who read my stories will be gripped by conviction and find the way of Jesus Christ. I do hope that God will use the stories to show the filthy heart of a man who recognizes and discloses layers of filth that is now covered by the forgiveness found by faith in Jesus Christ. I hope that many who read these stories will be relieved from guilt and shame because of the transparency and the open and frank admission of filth in my living contrary to the precepts of God. Further, I believe some who read my stories will be saved from wrongdoing and find hope.

Jimmy Swaggart was caught with a prostitute and exposed to the public. Cary John Efurd was not caught, but he broke the story to the public anyway. There is nothing more humiliating or cleansing as admitting to self, God, and another human being the exact nature of wrongs and then being willing to tell the story and make amends to the people harmed. There is nothing hidden from God. The truth of guilt and shame is never out of sight, always on the surface of emotion, and is a grievance to God's Holy Spirit, for as long as wrongdoing continues.

Admission of wrong is the beginning answer to any trespass. Knowing what is right and wrong is written in the Bible. We only come across God's will for our lives if we read the Bible and study and meditate on its words. Listening to sermons and songs like "The Old Rugged Cross" can help remind us. But it is we ourselves who have to take the steps to research our hearts and minds, discover our faults, admit our wrongs, and enact the willingness to follow instructions.

Before I stepped onto the yacht with Debby the night I asked her to marry me, "someday," I had months before been transparent with her about my promiscuous activities. I knew before telling her these things that I wanted Debby to marry me. It was an act of God working in me to find the courage. I wanted to have a clean heart in our relationship. We both had been married before. Together we decided to bring chasteness and honesty into our relationship. I believe that had I brought the darkest of my secrets into our marriage without the admission to myself, to God, and to her, Debby may not have said, "Yes, I will marry you someday." And we would not be the happiest of partners today. Remember, I have said that the day Debby and I said, "I do," she started on a path to face some of her most

48

difficult challenges. One challenge she has not had to face is unfaithfulness by her husband. Debby wrote our wedding vows. I said, "I do," to promise to love and honor her until death us do part.

I have fought three major battles over the last fifty-five years since I was saved in 1966: alcoholism, mental illness, and self. I believe my "self" has had the hell beat out of him by the love of God. The other two problems are taken care of by the doing. Today, it boils down to a simple question that I ask myself, *Who do I choose today, self or God?* Following after "self" is a game I play and never win.

Our transgressions are the dark spiritual foods that we can feed to the Holy Spirit. Let him have every morsel. Get rid of it! Pile it on His plate. The Holy Spirit cannot overeat. He is God. He will quickly make to disappear everything we bring to him. Even the best in us, he will make better.

We all belong to God, and he lives everywhere, even in our wrongs. He lives in hospitals, on the road to recovery, and as we run to and from "self." God does not like our actions of wrongdoing and less-than-virgin thoughts, but he never stops loving us. Accepting God's sovereign power and strength is the winning strategy. Willingness is the key that opens the door. May you find God now! He is as close as our next breath, if there be one.

Caution: being estranged from reality by mental illness may require professional help. I have had tons of professional counseling and treatment in hospitals for mental illness. All roads have led me to God. I am not perfect. I was not born to be perfect. I am not a professional. I live on a farm with cows and dogs. Amen.

The Blessed Life

It was in the years of 1999 and 2000, when I won trophies in power lifting competition. I was forty-six and forty-seven years old. When I tell people about it now, they look me over and say, really?

I say, "Yes, I was in the short, fat, bald-headed division," as I add, "Back then, I was a solid mass of rock."

I have noticed that the older I get, the better I was at everything (Read me lightly here and smile).

After the wreck of 1997, after the bankruptcy, after my second trip to TSH, and during the time I was working off my two-year sentence of community service for criminal homicide, reduced to negligent homicide at Straight Street Ministries, Cedar Hill, Texas, I joined a health club and began working on my physical condition.

At the gym is where I met Don. We became workout partners and the best of friends. In 2001, I stood beside Don as the best man at his wedding. Every morning, five days a week and twice on Saturdays, we'd meet at the gym at 4:30 a.m. for a two-hour workout before work. Don worked at Home Depot, and I had a job working for Century 21 Judge Fite Management Company. Don and I would alternate. One day we'd work on weights, and the next day we'd work on cardiovascular exercises. My starting weight was in the 240s. By my first competition, I topped in at 188 pounds. My age category for competing was forty-six to fifty-four. Don's age division was fifty-five and older. Don was fifty-five years old at the time. I was forty-six. Don was much stronger than I was. I only avoided having to compete with him because of the age difference. One significant thing I can say about Don and his strength and agility is that in prison, he had a lot of time to build muscle and endurance. He also built quality of character. God got a hold of Don, and Don never let God go.

A specific fact that speaks to me about Don, then, now, and going forward is that Don is the man who led me to begin tithing. He gifted me Robert Morris's series called *The Blessed Life*, in 2004. I have listened to the CDs hundreds of times, sometimes piecemeal and other times from beginning to end.

Don lived in Straight Street Ministries on a street named Straight Street, where I worked. The crime for which he was convicted somehow led him to the path of "the narrow way." I don't know *how* it happened. I can only talk about *what* happened.

Through Don and our teamwork to become power lifters, I became a "solid rock" of muscle, and also found "The Solid Rock" of tithing on which I stand. Had it not happened like it did, I don't believe I would be able to share anything about Jesus today. The love of money had always been a stronghold for me and can still be today. It could have been Don's stronghold too, but he's never said it to me. Thank you, Don, for the blessed life. Amen.

The Healing Process

It was May 15th, 1986. I was driving alone in some kind of car. I can't remember the make or model, but it was red and white color, looked kind of like a Maverick but had a hatch back. I think it was a Chrysler product. My kids called it "The Bumper Car," because I'd put 'em back there and make abrupt little turns back and forth going down the road. They'd giggle and laugh as they rolled around trying to stabilize themselves during the travel down the road.

This car that I bought for $3,000 was my most expensive possession. Burger Hausa had taken over C.J.'s Barbecue, and Fratellos Pizza and Game Room had already closed and had been made into a donut shop.

Alcohol and mental illness had been at the forefront of my life. This day in May of 1986 was a new day of freedom. Released from Terrell State, I was headed to my new home—a transition home in Dallas, Texas, where I would be living in a two-bedroom apartment with three other men and one million cockroaches. Maybe I have overshot that number of cockroaches by a few hundred thousand, but I'll say it like this: you could lay down a piece of toast and before the time it took to turn around, the roaches would have the toast covered.

My last home in Terrell State Hospital was looking pretty good in my estimation, at that point. Instead of alcohol, I bought Raid for cockroaches to celebrate my discharge from TSH. I offer tongue-in-cheek humor when I say now, that I graduated from Terrell State, that I am crazy, and I have the papers to prove it. It is true.

Still in the healing process, thirty-four years later, God is not through. It seems that I now have more boldness for Christ than I do for my "old self." I pray daily and sometimes moment-by-moment for my old self to be beaten down, in the name of Jesus, for the expansion of his Kingdom in this world. Amen.

Praying

Dear Lord,

I have been seeing and hearing on the news in past days and years that there is trouble in our nation, the United States of America. You have told us in your Word that "a house divided against itself cannot stand." Some people accept that the USA can go on without you in our schools, in our government, and in our homes. Some believe that the church is archaic and not necessary. They say we can survive without you. They say that you are a fictional being made up for the weak and feeble-minded. Others believe that you are the Way, the Truth and the Light, and nothing can survive without you.

Dear Lord,

Christians are being persecuted in our nation and around the world. People die from starvation and genocide every day. The pestilence of COVID-19 is causing sickness and death to our closest friends and neighbors. There is cancer, diabetes, and all sorts of other sickness plaguing us. In this twelve-o'clock hour on February 2, 2021, we pray for all of the people of these distinct divisions and illnesses. We pray especially for the people of the United States of America.

Dear Lord,

Your Scripture tells us that you led your children from captivity, out of the wilderness. You did not leave them to fall as waste. Your Scripture openly announced what we can see with our own eyes. There is profound immorality breeding in our nation. It seems to be overtaking us and even calling our names to submit to the evil. We are resisting, O God. We cry out to you with whimpering cries and loud voices for you to cause the U.S. (us) to recognize your authority and bring our nation yielded to your Word.

We do not pray these things with reservation to our prejudices, economic status, or political belief—Republican, Democrat, or otherwise. We come to you humbly as believers, and ask for your mercy and grace from our worries and resentments. We ask for you to supply what is lacking in our faith.

P. S.: Lord,

There are those among us who have tragically and unexpectedly lost their children to early deaths. Please attend to all of their sufferings immediately, and cause them to find peace and rest. For these things we ask as we lean on your everlasting arms that we may not fall away from unending prayer, in Jesus' name. Amen and amen.

John

Cognitive Therapy

When I was on "L" ward at Terrell State Hospital, I met a young man who was in his early twenties. This young man had completely torn out both of his eyeballs from their sockets. When asked how he could do such a thing, he cracked off, "Well, I inserted my forefingers and thumbs, grasped behind my eyeballs and yanked." He further chuckled, "I could not see what I had done." The question put forward by the group was intended for the young man to answer the question: "What was your motivation?"

I know this story is horrible. I have thought about the young man's declaration hundreds of times in my life since. If he is still living, he'd be in his late 50s. His claim he finally answered, as to why he did such a thing, was from Scripture—Matthew 18:9.

> *"If your eye causes you to stumble, gouge it out and throw it away. It is better for you to enter life with one eye than to have two eyes and be thrown into the fire of Hell."*

His diagnosis was bipolar.

A young woman on "L" went to the ladies' bathroom and used the tie of her bathrobe to hang herself from a stall's cross member that was attached to two partitions that held the partitions together. She was found and fortunately did not die. She was pretty, with a quick and smart mind.

Her diagnosis was bipolar with personality disorder.

56

A young man held a 22 revolver to the right frontal lobe area of his head and pulled the trigger. He did not die, but the impact of the bullet took out a chunk of his skull that remained noticeable at a glance. He was smart in mind, had a great personality, and was liked by everybody.

His diagnosis was depression.

Most of the women who wore long sleeves and high neck blouses or sweaters had image and eating disorders. They would use their fingernails to make long deep scratches on the inside of their forearms, neck, and torso.

The men and women of "L" ward were accomplished pianists, cellists, artists, electricians, mothers, fathers, carpenters, contractors—men and women from all walks of life.

What we all had been given on "L" ward were labels, which identified us in the hospital charts. Each diagnosis came with it the kind of medications we were prescribed. The charts had daily entries made by the hospital staff about how we were acting and what we had said. The charts were used by the psychiatrists and psychologists to help with treatment.

Part of treatment included writing in a journal. Every day I would write about my thoughts and give answers to questions that came out in daily group sessions usually led by the nurses of "L" ward and weekly community meetings led by the psychologists. I met with psychiatrists and psychologists after discharge until 1999. Now I go to my primary physician, who checks my blood levels for the medications I take for bipolar.

One of the ways that mental health workers evaluated my progress is by the way I answered questions. One of the most difficult questions for me to answer was when I'd say something or ask a question, and the psychiatrist, psychologist, or mental health staff worker would ask me, "What does that mean to you?" The question made me think, and it made me mad. Sometimes I hated to admit to the answer.

For me, one of the most important parts of treatment for mental illness is called "cognitive therapy." Cognitive therapy focuses on "present thinking." It's something I can do alone now, without an official therapy session, by asking myself, *What am I thinking about right now, why am I thinking it, and what does it mean to me?* Cognitive therapy has saved me a lot of grief, especially with relationships, but I still open my fat mouth and stick my foot in. Cognitive therapy is easy for me now when I do it. I am thinking right now about what I am saying in the post, what it may mean, and the reasons I am writing.

Caution: There was a time in my life that what I was thinking in the present did not have any constraints or perimeters of right and wrong. Any answer I gave myself could have sounded right, and the impulsiveness of my disease would have caused me to act. Think about the wreck that took the life of the young man. Think about the young man who yanked his eyeballs from his sockets with his justification being what the Bible said.

If you are having mental or emotional troubles of any kind, seek professional help. I am not a professional. All of the long process of recovery and seeming trouble was worth it to me. Since my mother and daddy had me committed and I was driven in a strait jacket to TSH, it has ultimately become my daily decision to continue with a mental and alcoholic recovery.

Think about this present moment in which we are living. What does it mean?

Dear Lord,

There are many things we hold in our minds. We have grown up in a variety of fashions. We hold precious thoughts of our loved ones and friends. We are living in difficulty accepting the ways of many we know. If there is one thing that is true, it is you. You have promised to care for us and deliver us from mental anguish, wrong thoughts, and wrongdoings. I expect a swift answer to this prayer. Lord over us and send the help we need.

In Jesus' name. Amen.

Cheating

I cheated my way through high school, not totally, but mostly. I looked across the aisle with strained vision. I created cheat sheets that fit in the palm of my hand. I wrote on the palm of my hand. I wrote on the desk I was sitting in.

I was so intent on making a passing grade that one time I stood and leaned straight up in my desk, in full display of the teacher, and looked over the shoulder of the person sitting in front of me. I was caught by the teacher and embarrassed in front of the others in the class as she asked, "Cary John, what do you think you are doing?"

If the smartest person in class was not sitting nearby, I'd cheat off the dumbest person nearby. I cheated in bookkeeping, spelling, history, and English. I made the same grade and missed the same questions as the classmates I was copying and cheating until I learned that I needed to change a few of the answers to make my grade different. I had started drinking by then.

In elementary and through junior high, I had made near-perfect grades. Thank God I learned to read, write, add, and subtract before I started drinking.

There is something about the effect of alcohol on a young mind, or any mind for that matter. An alcoholic mind thinks differently. Just as I hid answers for a test and my cheating, so this alcoholic hid his "bottle" (and drugs). I hid them from my true self, my wife, my employees, my children, the preacher, and all the people I knew who would condemn me if they found out. It's crazy! It's cheating, and I cheated for many years.

I have learned that I was only cheating myself. The people from whom I was hiding may have condemned me, but I had already condemned myself. A decision to continue cheating and hiding was senseless. I was damned if I did and damned if I didn't. I could not live without alcohol, and I could no longer continue to live with it.

Ten thousand words from other people could not turn me. It took only one word: God. Seeking him was the answer. Look! He is not lost. Praise God, in the name of Jesus, amen.

My mother wrote my sophomore English theme on the same dining room table, in the same house that Debby and I use and where we live today. She made an A in my name as she prayed the name of Jesus to lord over my life.

Empty Containers

A day of writing is like a day of sunshine on a cloudy day. The clouds are dark and the sky is gray, but "I got sunshine on a cloudy day." The Temptations were dynamic performers and became one of the most successful groups in popular music. The deaths of the members are mostly tragic:

- Melvin Franklin, age fifty-two, was shot protecting his car from being stolen, and his subsequent drug use led to serious health issues.
- Paul Williams, age thirty-four, committed suicide after leaving his new house and an argument with his girlfriend.
- David Ruffin, age fifty, collapsed and died at a crack cocaine drug house.
- Eddie Kendricks, age fifty-two, died of lung cancer due to thirty years of smoking.
- Otis Williams, born in Texarkana, Texas, is seventy-nine years old at the time of this writing and is still performing.

Elvis sang about fame and fortune and "How empty they can be." Elvis died at the age of forty-two, reportedly of a drug overdose. Maybe it was fame and fortune that killed him. I can't say. I'll call Elvis the most famous and outstanding entertainer who ever set foot on a stage with a microphone and sang a song, gave away a Cadillac, used drugs, had affairs and starred in thirty-one movies. You may contest me, but I will not be moved.

Empty beer cans and empty whiskey bottles, empty pipes for smoking crack cocaine—empty paraphernalia of any kind leave voids in the heart, mind, and soul of man and empty relationships that Fame and Fortune cannot fill. Only God can fill that void. The man writing these words found hope in God, who allowed him to live through his experiences and find strength.

Containers that held the supply to feed my alcohol addiction could never hold enough. The containers were always empty. I used to sit on "L" ward and imagine how much alcohol I had drunk in eighteen years and how much money my drinking had cost me (as well as my mother and dad). I cannot begin to estimate a calculation, but I am sure that the empty containers would fill some size of a large warehouse and the cost of the alcohol itself would at minimum have paid my way through college. The lost income could be astronomical in wasted time, lost wages, costs of the DWIs' lost opportunity, lost relationships, so forth and so on and more. The gross amount of money that I have earned since 1985, including the years I worked in high school for a bricklayer, making $3.65 per hour, as a painter making nothing, the time digging ditches making $6–7 an hour, working at Pitt Grill for $5.25 per hour, filing for bankruptcy and starting over, building a property management company that Debby and I sold in 2017, is estimated in the millions. Debby and I have given away more than we have and still have more than we ever dreamed possible. Enough by the grace of God! Everything is made by God and belongs to God. He owns the cattle on a thousand hills.

Lord,

We come to you empty and broken in heart, mind and soul. Some of us have bodies that are broken. We bathe our brokenness with your comforting words of power and find strength to carry on as a witness to the saving grace and power of Jesus, your Son. In him we pray. Amen.

Filling the Void

Imagine the day without the sun, night without the stars, the winter without the wind, the cold without its chill, heat without the hot. What if there were no tomorrow, and we knew this was our last day? What if our eyes could see that all we need is what we have?

It was 1975, after my academic expulsion from college the previous year and after having spent the winter pruning peach trees with my dad. I opened Cary John Efurd's Fratello's Pizza Parlor on Greer Boulevard in Pittsburg, Texas. I had to get my name on the sign to be like my grand d Cary J. Martin of Texas. How many gas stations do you think would be behind a name like that, 20–30? There was one. Grandiosity. Papaw may have been touched with bipolar too. They say it runs in the family.

With my grandfather's financial support, I took over ownership from my grandfather's friend, Wayne Shellnut. Wayne had been operating Fratello's Pizza Parlor but was forced to close down because of health issues. Wayne spent about two weeks with me, showing me the ins and outs of making pizza, subs, and salads. I was energized enough to quit, slow down, and hide my drinking for a couple of years, but I began smoking more "pot," marijuana, cannabis . . . I'd roll a "joint," "take a toke."

The pizza parlor did pretty good for a small-town business. It became a hangout for the schoolboys in town. There was foosball, pinball, video games, and pool. Everything was quarter-slot play.

My high school sweetheart got married in February of 1976, and by May of that year, I was married, too My high school sweetheart had left me in college because of my propensity to drink alcohol. She was smart to get away from me. I see it now.

My new wife was my sweetheart too. Our marriage lasted six years before I destroyed any hope she had for our marriage and family. She sent me packing via divorce. I had begun having manic (bipolar) episodes and drinking alcohol to self-alleviate the depression. We had two kids. I was never home. I had to work, play, and hide in the bottle from the darkness of my soul.

For those who are still suffering: I was always trying to fill the "void" that is so famously talked about in self-help circles, by psychiatrists, in AA, and in some pulpits. The void, the hole, the missing "something" can't be plugged, no matter how many women, drinks, tokes, smokes, huffs, main-line punctures with a needle, or the number of times you cry out to God Almighty to save you. It will never happen unless you admit first to your innermost self that you have had enough.

If you are anything at all like me, you will recognize what I am saying is true. If you don't understand, then you are either not ready, in denial, or you don't have a problem. If you don't have a problem, but are a participant in using drugs and alcohol, I say try stopping for a month. Try stopping for a week. Stay sober for a year, then another. Try proving to yourself that you can go without your substance of choice, get a job, go home to your wife, be civil to your parents, save your money, make payments on your car. You don't have to "white knuckle" sobriety. There is everything right about getting help. Going it alone is hard. It can be done, but it is not necessary. We are a prideful lot, the kind of pride that goes before a fall.

Everybody that finds themselves in the dark places understands despair. Without despair, we wouldn't have a need to

66

get drunk, stoned, high, and try to escape from ourselves by the use of downers, uppers, scotch, ale, meth, cocaine, heroin, and more. It's just that simple.

It is just as simple to understand that an addict/alcoholic may not be able to say no to all of the above the next time we are up against the wall, trying to run from ourselves and blaming our problems on everybody, on everything, but the decisions we have made for ourselves, on our own. Do you know what I am talking about? How many times have you been in jail, prison, been broke (I bet you are now), fired, divorced, never married, etc.—all because you weren't trustworthy, honest, responsible, reasonable, nice, happy, glad, and grateful for what you have. If you recognize that you need help, seek it, now!

What if there were no tomorrow, and we knew this was our last day? What if our eyes could see that all we need is what we have?

I don't know what came first, the chicken or the egg. But long ago in the summer of 1967, I made a choice to be somebody else, to be who I wasn't, for who knows what reasons. Was it because I was short, pudgy, had an overbite, wore braces that glinted in the sun when I smiled? Was it because I didn't have the popularity that others had, worried if I was saved or not, or because my folks didn't have the money that some of my friends had? Was it because I felt guilty for being naughty and not nice? Would it be Heaven or Hell for me? It does not matter what the reasons were. I chose Hell and ended up in "L," the place I needed to be.

Lord,

Take our emptiness and fill us with your love and glory. Praise goes to you for your mercy to the suffering. In Jesus name, amen.

The Best Medicine

The kind of book that I want to write is one that has an immediate and lasting impact on the people who God made. We are the people God made—all of us: all people, black, white, red and brown, crippled and maimed, the sick and dying. A book like I describe has already been written. It is called the Bible. I pray that you will find it now, dust it off, pick it up, take it out of your car, and remember to bring it back to church with you next Sunday. Open it to any page, chapter, or verse and start reading, studying, meditating, believing in its truth, and living by it as your plan for relief from every sorrow, sadness, and pain. Receive its promises of joy, strength, hope, and a life that will not end here on this earth. You and I will live for a billion years after we leave this earth and then we will have only just begun.

Many people—drug addicts, alcoholics, child traffickers, family abusers—have an aversion to hearing anything about the glory of God and his love. These people, and I was one of them, do not believe they are worthy of love or forgiveness. They believe they have gone too far, been separated too long by living in an alternate world to ever have a chance at life again. A simplification of the problem is the cloud, darkness, hardness, of the heart mind and soul. They cannot see or hear anything but the next thought that comes into their mind. What always came first into my mind was despair that led to depression, which led to the use of the substance that fueled my addiction. It was a never-ending circle, but it did finally end. I found hope in Jesus Christ and made him Lord of my life, with new thoughts, healing thoughts that came to life in my life. This life is available to everybody, all of us, everyone.

I will never be able to write a book like the Bible. Please pray with me, that *To L and Back* may be stumbled upon by many suffering souls and it will help lead them to the saving power of Christ Jesus and to the whole truth, which is nothing but the truth, the Bible, God's Holy Word.

There is a name I love to hear. It starts with a "J" and has five syllables. You can pronounce it correctly by following these instructions. Say, Jay, then a long vowel "A," say two "R's" combined with an "E." Hold it there, and sing out for the count of two whole notes, make the "Y" silent, then rest, and say Jareeeee! That's what his mother called him when she called him in for lunch—possum and turnip greens. Sometimes she'd call him. "You've Had Enough."

Jerry is a professional comedian who is still one of my best friends. He is well known in the East Texas towns around and is one of the most loved of all people in Pittsburg, Texas. He lived up to his famous personality traits that gained him the esteemed honor of All School Favorite in high school, along with another of my friends, Co-favorite, Brian, who became famous in acting, dance productions, TV, and movies. Brian's fame comes from all who know him locally and in European countries, especially Italy. I love them both, and both are talented and funny people.

Jerry has been making me laugh since the first grade, when we were lying on our mats for nap time and I saw him float a feather (pulled from his nap mat) up the teacher's dress as she stepped across the floor furnace. It must have been about February of 1960. Jerry taught me all I knew about first-grade girls: "Stay away from them. They have girl germs." Jerry is as funny as Tim Allen, Bill Murray, and Jerry Seinfeld, but his humor is clean like Jerry Clower's. If you have every belly-laughed at one of Jerry's performances, you know what I am saying is true. Jerry's stage name is "Buck," a nickname his mother didn't give him.

"Laughter is the Best Medicine." That's a category found in *The Readers Digest*. What's not read in *The Reader's Digest* is that laughter can stop a bullet. Laughter can stop the "bullet" of our sufferings that we "mainline," hold on to, allow to linger, obsess over, are excessively preoccupied with, fixated upon, or allow to haunt us. These are the "bullets" that tell us we are not worthy, because we were born into poverty, grew up without a father or mother, were adopted, lost our jobs, our money, or our reason for living. The list goes on: kids in prison, children lost to drugs and alcohol abuse, to prison because of thievery, dealing drugs, and more. Anything that we despise and grieve over without Christ as the center of our lives will quench, snuff out, extinguish, stamp out, smother, put out, blow out and douse the Holy Spirit of God inside of us. We must clear away all of that and make it the "wreckage of our past," nothing more. We must come to see that all of what we have lived through becomes our prayer to Jesus and testament to others who are suffering with the same— that how we live today is the hope that others will see is the love of God.

God is in charge of the salvation of our souls. We are in charge of giving our souls to the comfort of his love. Our children, our family and friends—we all have been given the same opportunity in a present and continuing form to accept his love

In 1977, I opened C.J.'s Barbecue, across the street from Cary John Efurd Fratello's Pizza. It had been a barbecue place for about seven years and was named Watson's Barbecue. I purchased the business, and I can't really remember how much I paid or how I paid for it. It seems like I paid $7,000 for the business, the equipment, and the right to move into the building and paid $700 a month rent to Mrs. Watson. My grandfather had been murdered in 1975. He wasn't there to help me. Maybe I had a little money saved. Maybe Chuck let me pay it out, or maybe my mother and dad helped.

It wasn't long before the business flourished. We were catering large events like Ducks Unlimited, Chamber of Commerce banquets, rehearsal dinners, outdoor gatherings, and more. We fed both the Lions Club and Rotary Club for their weekly meetings. I purchased a "roach coach" and hired a pretty girl to run routes to industrial and construction sites. My brother-in-law helped me build a covered wagon that we used for onsite events and for selling barbecue at events such as Pioneer Days. I had a refrigerator back by the barbecue pit, where I kept cold beer. I checked on the meat often.

I had it all—two businesses, a beautiful family and wife, a little boy and a little girl on the way, and money was coming in. I purchased a house. I had it all. None of it would last.

I have a recurring dream. Maybe it stems from me not wanting to be found out. The dream consists of me wearing overalls and a C. J.'s hat, lying on my right side on the floor, facing the door at the barbecue place, looking and greeting people coming in, and believing they may not notice me on the floor drunk if I could just give them a friendly smile.

To the sufferer, the bottom line is this: You are not going to get away with it. You will end in disgrace. You will not make it out alive. You will die by your on hand, one way or another. Without help, you will have a tragic and untimely death. You may be found dead, floating in a river, dumped over the bridge over a dealer's debt. You may die by someone's hand in prison. You may crash into a bridge while driving from a drinkers' club. You may die lain waste by a liver that stopped you in your tracks. By your own hand, it will happen. You must concede. You must surrender to win the battle of addiction and abuse.

Surrender to God and his saving power. It may take a commitment to a hospital, but certainly there must be an ultimate commitment to God. Do it now! Hospitals and prisons are good places to get started. At least you are off the streets, can dry up, sober up, clean up, and clear your mind to think and pray and read and start anew every day, in the fresh, loving presence of God Almighty.

There is hope. The hope is what we hear when we are alone. Hope speaks in the desperate sounds of our innermost cries of hopelessness. The sound you hear in desperation is Jesus speaking. It is the sound of his Holy Spirit still alive in you. It is God calling your name, because he has plans for you. He wants to help you. He is fighting to save you. It is his voice in the pain you feel. He is grieving and speaking as you grieve. Be still and know that he is God. Be still. He is calling!

Jesus suffered the pain for you on the cross. It is for your pain he suffered on the cross. If you don't surrender while there is time, the pain on this earth will continue to be hell on earth. I don't know if you are saved or not. That's between you and Jesus. A lot of people who live a life of addiction are saved. If you are not, and know you are not, say this prayer:

Jesus, come to me in my pain and suffering. Relieve me of the bondage of myself, my addiction. If you will accept me, Lord, I will accept you.

If you said that prayer and you were sincere, welcome to the Kingdom of God and life eternal. The next step is to get into his Word, get into treatment, and let your life become a living testimony to the saving power of Jesus Christ. In his name I pray. Amen.

It's not the drugs and alcohol that call out to us. It is the pain and shame inside that is convicting us of a shallow life. Conviction is the loving grace of God that is speaking to us to surrender our lives over to the care of God in the best way we can understand him. His glory will prevail and his most high redemption will bring us home to the people he wants us to be.

We know why we drug and drink. It is for every reason in the world we can think of. Any time and any reason are good times to abuse ourselves. I heard of a man whose skull stopped a bullet. He died. The best that could be determined without a note was that the wind had blown his open paint bucket off the ladder onto the ground. He died because the wind blew.

Laughter is the best medicine. In AA it's said that we should wear the world like a loose garment, plenty of room to move around, not too tight. There is no shame in laughing at the stupid things we do.

Lord,

You are the Maker and Ruler of all things. We have a mind and we have a choice. You gave us our mind and you gave us our free will. We come to you asking for the benefits of your Holy Spirit to come inside our hearts and minds and grace us with your presence.

On Trial

God our Savior, Master, and Lord lives in the smallest, finest, littlest, most minuscule, insignificant, biggest, largest, most huge, mountainous, disruptive—the frequent interruptions, all concerns and joys, in every part of our lives and existence, the universe included. He lives! Amen and hallelujah! He lives.

After the wreck in October of 1997 that killed a young man (Gabriel), I was sued for damages by the departed man's wife and family. I had been processed through the grand jury, charged for criminal negligent homicide, and would be tried for a crime, substantially delivered by the hand of mental illness. I was driving the vehicle. Mental illness, untreated, was the navigator, sadly.

I hadn't long been released from my second state-funded commitment to Terrell State Hospital, where I had been placed in a holding ward with no treatment. I was held for thirty days awaiting trial. Debby and I were separated. An attack of severe stress and strain assailed us. It was God in us that saw us through the massive, largest, most huge, disruptive, mountainous challenge of our marriage. In times of stress, distress, trouble, death and pain, God, yes, he is there living inside of our hearts, minds, and souls to carry us through. He lives everywhere, all around, up and down, left and right, and for all time does he live! Amen.

When Debby and I got to court, the room was full, packed, brimming. We were in tight quarters with the loving, kind, caring, praying, devoted people of God who were members and friends of the church Debby and I attended.

My attorney had prepared three witnesses to speak on my behalf. God, with the pastor of our church, had brought the multitudes to fill courtroom pews, sit, listen, and pray. I had not expected to see all the people! What I saw, I will never forget: a generous, undeserving, show of love and support. It was God in the people, him in the pews. He is here now in a healing moment. Forevermore, he is here!

There were other people in the courtroom pews. There was Gabriel's wife, his father, his mother, brother, and sister. There was Gabriel's wife's mother, her father, her brothers and sisters, family and friends. The sight of them took my breath away as I faced them from the witness stand. We, the saved and unsaved, all will be on the witness stand before Christ's judgment seat one day, after our last breath is taken on Earth. What will our breath deliver to God in answer to his questions?

The three witnesses my attorney prepared went first. Then it was my turn. There was not much that I could say to the attorneys and the judge except, "Yes, I was the one driving the car that killed Gabriel." After I was through testifying, and before stepping down from the stand, I turned to the judge and asked him to allow me to read a letter I had prepared for Gabriel's wife. The words were blurred by the tears in my eyes. Gabriel's wife was crying as I read to her: Gabriel's last words to me were, *"Tell my wife I love her. Promise me you will tell her."*

Amen.

First Place

I have been arrested, jailed, asylumed, worried, failed in business, failed in grades, been bankrupt, divorced; had manic episodes, and have been depressed; suicidal, unloving, unkind. I have also been kind, joyous, free from worry, thoughtful, and happy to be alive. I have been a bad father, a good father; a bad husband, a good husband.

I am at my best with the Holy Spirit's guidance. We all are. As truth prevails, we all will be freed from all doubt. For the nonbeliever, God has a purpose for you. God's purpose is more glorious, more star-studded, more holy, better than the best dreams you have ever had for yourself, more of anything and everything you may imagine. He calls your name. You are his. He made you. He formed you in your mother's womb to be you, the best you that you can be. Go to him in Romans 10:13, and keep reading. By belief in him, you have purpose.

Nothing can happen without God ordaining it. Psalm 57:2 says, "I cry out to God Most High, to God, who vindicates me. This word from the Most Holy God should be eye opening for all of us.

There is no way around it. God has a purpose for us. Even in our disbelief, unbelief, and denial, truth remains. The question has been answered. There is a purpose for our being. Can we run and hide? Running and hiding causes unsatisfactory, less-than-desirable results and more grief than we want to bear and may have already borne. Without God, our griefs are not over. The answer is no, we cannot run and hide. We can only try.

God has numbered our days. He will fulfill every purpose he has for us in our lifetime. How can God fulfill every purpose he has for us if we don't feel like it, don't want it? How can God fulfill every purpose if our life is full of pain, regret, disaster, sorrow? How can God fulfill every purpose if we work in a job we hate, drink like there were no tomorrow, try to find relief in

76

drugs, alcohol and sex? The answer is that God wants us to love him first, above all else, above all things—more than money, power, and fame.

He must be first above success in our career and before the love of our children. He wants us to put him first in our work place, first in our marriages, first in the way we treat others. Putting God first allows us to do the hard things easily: love our enemies, forgive our debtors, resist temptation, recognize our weaknesses and become strong to say no to our free will and yes to the will of God. He is more powerful than the battering ram of our foes.

God will not accept second place. Yes, above all else, God wants our devotion. Love of God is the beginning. Love of him is the ending. He is the beginning and the end, Alpha and Omega.

If God is not first, we find no real joy in our work. Our family life is less than flattering, both inside and outside the home. Our fake belief becomes make-believe. Only with him being first place in our lives can we find joy in another person, place, or thing.

Dependence on people, places and things, heroes, hobbies, and clothing all quickly fade. We will need more, and we will never be filled with them. The God of joy, God of love, God of peace, God of hope is the filling and lasting way. There is only one choice. The Way, the Truth, and the Light—Jesus. Amen.

What are you feeling, believing, seeing in your life as you have read these words? If there is fulfillment, I believe God has made it so for you. Is there doubt? He is causing that too. He is calling you to come home. He calls all of us home, all of the time and always, never ending, everlasting. He is our Father. We are his children. Acceptance of the truth satisfies every need and gives strength to enjoy every day, every task, every loved one. Acceptance of the truth makes good our every disappointment, every failure, every time. Submission to God and obedience to his word equal purpose in life.

Today, a pipe burst under my house from the freezing temperatures we have been enjoying (an act of God). I had choices. I could shut off the main water supply and have no water in the house. I could let it go and let water and freezing temperatures create a skating rink in my back yard, or I could crawl under the house and see if there was anything I could do.

This happened last evening, Wednesday, February 16, 2020, at about 8:00 p.m., while I was watching an episode of *Criminal Minds* (I prefer *Green Acres.*) I called out to Debby, engaging her in this one-man job, asking her, "Where are my warm coveralls?"

Debby is always able to tell me where everything is, even the stuff that I lose right in front of my eyes and things lost and out of sight. I don't know how she does it.

I suited up with my very best, warmest attire, including a toboggan that had a mounted LED light. I laced up my high shaft boots and headed off to the pole barn for a drill motor. Returning, I turned on my toboggan's head light, used the motor and star bit to remove the cover from the opening to the crawl space, got down on my knees, laid flat on my fat stomach (I was not exactly flat). There was some elevation.

I began to crawl. I immediately saw a stream of water flowing, making its way from the center of the house, following its self-made path along the east wall of the house, going under the back porch deck, and onto the back yard. I could not yet see the source. I dragged myself along by elbows and knees, using my stomach too.

Presently, I could hear a water sound that was not unlike the sound heard by water coming from a water hose filling up an inflatable swimming pool or a five-gallon bucket. In fact, it sounded just like that. Chugging along at a turtle's pace, at about thirty feet in from where I started, my toboggan light glistened onto water coming from a ½" copper line that had come loose at a joint. I could tell immediately that there would be no repair made that night. I inched along toward the source, about ten feet farther. I was now close enough that, had the source been a book, I could have read it.

I was able to see clearly. I could see steam piping up as hot water coming from the line was condensed by the cold air. I knew then that the broken water line was connected to the water heater inside the house. I backed up, turned around and wormed my way back out.

Inside the house, I shut off the water supply to the water heater. Water stopped running under the house. Debby was there with me, at first outside on the porch as I started my crawl, then peering through the open window so she could hear if I called for help. Debby and I both agreed that cold water is better than no water. We are grateful for a flushing toilet too. Life is good.

There is joy in the untimely, unglamourous, holy-cow-what's-happened events of life. Going to the source, we find all answers and purpose.

Tittle and Iotas

God isn't just interested in our life as a whole. He cares about every single detail, the tittles and iotas—even the look on our face, the smile, the frown, the scowl, and the grins. We cannot shut him out. He is everywhere. He made everything. He holds us, keeps us, gives to us, forgives us, and somehow finds time to make a bankruptcy hearing.

In the spring of 1997, before the accident, before bankruptcy, before mania took hold of my life again, I was in downtown Dallas having just dropped Debby off for work. People were bustling around. Traffic was slow.

Having just turned right off of Griffin Street onto Commerce Street, I saw a young woman who I had not seen since her graduation from college at Southern Methodist University, some twenty years prior. I pulled my car slightly right, angling toward the curb, stopped and called out her name through the passenger-side window.

She came to the window in surprise of seeing me.

We exchanged niceties to each other, but the heart of the conversation came to the many years of "best friend" relationship she had with my ex-sister-in-law. I had known somehow that their "best friend" relationship no longer held fervor. I don't know why the relationship had ended, but in that moment, I somehow knew that I was supposed to say these parting words to the *summa cum laude* graduate, now lawyer: "I know that your friend would love to hear from you."

The final words from her to me as I began to pull back into traffic were: "I will call her."

I found out that she did call. The relationship rekindled and carries on today.

One year later, in May of 1998, the tragic accident had happened. I had spent thirty days in Terrell State Hospital. The court hearing for the accident was over. Debby and I had liquidated our business, sold our real estate assets, and filed for a Chapter 7 bankruptcy. We were now in the Earl Campbell Federal building for the bankruptcy hearing.

Debby and I were in debt for tens of thousands of dollars. I was not employed. Debby was working on a new job. We had been briefed by the attorney who filed the bankruptcy in what we could expect—a series of questions. I remember that we would need to answer no to all the questions for the Chapter 7 to be allowed.

At the moment before the first question was asked, the *summa cum laude* attorney I had spoken to on the corner of Field and Commerce the year before, leaned into the doorway and said, "Excuse me, your honor, may I come in and give the debtor a hug." She came in, hugged me, spoke to Debby, said thank you to the trustee, and walked out. With that, in less than a minute of time, the hearing concluded. No questions. Amen.

A Life Story to Tell

It was October 1, 1997. I had not yet been arrested, but I was in custody, having been taken from the site of the wreck to Parkland Hospital by Dallas police, where I would be treated for second- and third-degree burns to my hands and forearms.

Two officers came into the treatment room where I was admitted. They asked me to stand up, look straight into their flashlight. "Look left, look right, look up, and look down." My eyes followed the tip of a ballpoint pen, moving to said directions. After the officers' investigation for sobriety, I heard one of them tell the other, "I see no evidence of drugs or alcohol."

That conclusion was by the grace of God and only the grace of God. I believe that fact saved me from prison time. I know it did, not that I shouldn't have deserved prison.

After the officers left the room, I was alone. Impervious to physical pain as it is in full-blown mania, I began a process of peeling, pulling and jerking away the melted skin from my upper extremities, the palms of my hands, the backs of my hands, the tips of my fingers, around every cuticle, past my wrists to my forearms, up midway to my elbows. I removed every evidence that I had been burned except for the exposed blood-flushed red and pink color of raw skin.

I looked it up and found that humans have seven layers of skin. Gabriel had to have been burned with fourth-, fifth-, sixth- and seventh-degree burns over his entire body. It makes me sick to think about it, as I write here and now. Praise God for his mercy and grace. I can only believe that God saved me for a reason, and he had a reason that he wanted Gabriel to die at my hand. God is using Gabriel's life to help me tell you this story. It doesn't seem fair, but until God calls me home, I will be telling others about the deaths of Gabriel and Jesus. Have you thought about the agonizing death of Jesus lately?

When a nurse came in, she inspected the burned areas and commented on what a good job I did cleaning. She only had to apply antiseptic and dress the burns with Silva and gauze bandages.

After the nurse left, I stepped out the door and walked down the hall to the corner of another hallway. Looking to the right, I saw a woman police officer standing akimbo near a gurney. I knew instinctively that she was in front of the room where Gabriel was being treated.

The inhibition of fear gave way to boldness, as had happened at other times. I approached the officer and began asking about Gabriel's condition. This moment is when I found out his name. The officer said, "Gabriel is in serious condition."

I told her with hope, "He is going to be okay."

With assurance, she said sadly, "No, I don't think he will."

The officer and I had a conversation with her asking me questions. She was looking for a confession of wrongdoing. I kept to the fact that I was driving too fast. A manic depressive can make you believe he is perfectly fine, all the while being sick beyond belief.

I was sent to Green Oaks Hospital in Dallas. There was a psych ward there.

I could pull myself into proper behavior at will. It is like putting on a disguise. It is part of the invincibility aspect of the illness, winning against all odds. After two nights in Green Oaks, I was taken back to Parkland and released alone in front of the hospital. I was there to see a doctor. I went into the lobby and sat on a waiting bench. I started talking to the receptionists. I was gracious and in good behavior.

I was cracking jokes, and they were disarmed from any worry about my behavior or mental condition. I excused myself and went to the men's restroom. I don't know if it was impulsive or compulsive or both, but I yanked the lavatory off the wall and then disjointed the commode from the floor. There was a flood, and the police were called. I was charged for destruction of property and assault. I was restrained and taken upstairs in handcuffs.

My wife was called. She had been driven to work by my construction manager, James.

James picked Debby up from work and drove her to the hospital. On the way Debby called our pastor. By the time my pastor got there, I was in full manic rage.

I was being held down on the floor by three men with a fourth man straddling my chest with both of his hands choking my throat. I remember not being able to breathe. I was spewing out expletives. It was !!!?? this and !!!?? that and all of the rest of the ugly words you hear on television and in movies today.

My pastor stayed with me, talking to me, pleading at times. An officer was trying to unlock the final cuff from my right wrist. I was in rage. He was having trouble. The male nurse straddling my chest continued to choke me. It was deliberate. I believed he was trying to keep me from breathing.

I said to him, "As soon as I am free from these handcuffs, I am going to punch you square in the nose, you blankety-blank-blank."

At the moment I said blanket-blank-blank, the final cuff came off, and my right arm was free. With clinched hand by relief of the restraint, I hit the man squarely in the nose with the power of manic-enraged adrenaline. I could feel and hear his nose break and saw blood dripping onto my shirt through the voids of his cupped hands then covering his nose and face.

84

I was quickly subdued by the staff of the hospital and officers of the city, then placed in a holding cell of Parkland Hospital. I was later charged with felony assault. There is no doubt that mania is a powerful force, and combined with the force of a human will, it can overpower the greatest of odds.

A person in a manic episode is not unlike the narcissist in one sense: he cannot see his illness and doesn't want to see it. He or she is never wrong and blames others. Others are stupid. In the depressive side of the bipolar illness, the person knows there is something wrong but does not understand what is wrong. He typically wants to die, or at minimum hates his life with suffering and passionate emotion. Manic depressives live off the spectrum of being a normal person. Remembering details with exactness is a phenomenon of the bipolar nature.

For an active manic-depressive person, inhibitions are always in second place to bad behavior. Sometimes all moral restraints are vanquished. Living through a manic episode is a losing proposition for everybody involved. If not losing, it is certainly horrific, which is still losing.

I am telling you, the sufferer, with prayer that you will hear. You probably drink alcohol excessively, maybe use drugs, and certainly are a threat to others. You may not act with malice, but you are certainly an accident waiting to happen, a walking time bomb for destruction in your relationships, with acquaintances and people with whom you do business. Your money is at risk, and so is your employment. I could go on. Some, if not all in the list, have probably already happened to you. Get some help. It's not too late. Walk, run, fall down, and beg for help.

There is another truth about the bipolar individual. He will often throw himself heavily into either politics or religion and sometimes both. This is another warning signal. The difference between the bipolar interest in God and a personal relationship with God for the normal Christian is as the bipolar would say, "I am right, and you are wrong." Politics is the same. Sometimes I experienced both religious and political bents.

If you are a sufferer of bipolar and still reading, it may seem that I am overstating some things. I know you are smart and wise when you think other people are trying to tell you something you don't want to hear, but I know it takes a lot for us bipolar people to come to our senses. You don't have to go any further.

In mania, being out of control is normal behavior. Being in control and seeming normal is normal behavior for manic depressives too, but all behavior of an active manic depressive is out-of-control behavior. It is raw behavior without inhibitions, raw deceit by skirting the edges of truth. Mania, the kind that comes with the bipolar or manic-depressive illness, causes the most terrible kinds of turmoil, disaster, upset, criminal behavior, and unrestrained inhibitions.

God takes us the way we are. We have a choice. Even in mental illness, he is with us. He will save us, or he will let us die or go to prison. We have a choice. We have a life story to tell. God wants us to use our life stories to bring others to his saving grace. He has called us, all of us, to tell our stories of victory in Jesus. It is on his command that we tell the world about him and his saving grace. Amen.

New Year's Eve

Someone asked me if I have regrets for the terrible events of my life. My answer is no. If I did, I would be living in regret forever and a day. God doesn't want that for any of us.

How could I rectify killing a nineteen-year-old boy who had a young wife and an eight-month-old baby son? How could saying I am sorry ever be enough to pay the debt? How could I ever have enough regret for the terror I caused the jailer who was just doing his job in 1984? It is impossible to have that much regret.

Unending regret leads to substance abuse, mental illness, and suicide. In AA, we learn that we do not regret our past nor wish to shut the door on it. We see how our experience, strength, and hope found in recovery from mistakes, wrongdoings, criminal activity, alcohol, and drug abuse can be used to help others.

I was reported to the police by the manager of Tiffany's, a dance club and bar in Mount Pleasant, Texas. It was on the evening of December 30, 1984. I was taken and confined in the Titus County jail, having been arrested for disturbing the peace. I was in a manic episode. No alcohol was involved.

When I saw the police pull up to the back entrance of Tiffany's, I innately knew they had come for me. In a moment, in the twinkling of an eye, my behavior changed from disruptive to peaceful. There were no fights or altercations. It is a fact, however, that I was working as a self-appointed employee of Tiffany's in the capacity of greeter and doorman. The manager asked me to quit, and I wouldn't. Maybe I would have quit if he had threatened to fire me.

The police did not handcuff me. They did not lay a hand on me. The police said they wanted to take me with them, then opened the back door of the squad car, and I got in. On the way to jail, the lawmen asked me various questions about drinking and drugs, where I was from and who my family was. I remember a cringe of shame when I told them my mother and father were Sandra and John Hart Efurd. The police knew of Efurd Orchards. Efurd is a well-known brand name in the area for peaches, produce, and homemade ice cream.

The Efurd name may have preempted a usual and normal intake of me by the jailer, or it could have been that my peace act was working. It happened just like this: The jailer took my wallet, looked at my driver's license, wrote down the license number, and handed back my wallet—nothing more. I was not searched for drugs, guns, knives, or given a breathalyzer test. I was just put in a room made of concrete and bars, with a door that required a key to open. It was about ten o'clock, two hours before New Year's Eve.

The cell at the county jail had a built-in concrete bed jutting from the west wall. There was a wool blanket, and a thin, flat pillow on the bed. A soiled ceramic toilet stood alone on the south wall. There was no lavatory. Above the toilet, as high as the ceiling, was a small vented window protected by metal bars.

Through the vented window came melodies of the Christmas season chimed by the tower bells of the county court house across the street. The refrain of "Silent Night" filled my ears and my cell. My mania spoke to me, saying, "Piped-in music, just for me!" On the concrete wall, where the bed was, could be seen another single row of bars, vertical and evenly spaced as part of the wall that partitioned my cell from the next. The bars descended about two feet down from the ceiling and spanned the

88

length of the wall. The size of the cell was about eight-foot square.

Mania, a form of self will without the fear of consequences, is fierce and reveals unsuspecting deeds of disruption. Everything I did was done by me and for my good pleasure. I was wearing a gray pullover hooded sweater, one with those feel-through pockets in front for carrying things and hand warming. The jailer's failure to search left me with seven Black Cat firecrackers, a pack of "close the cover before striking" matches with seven red-tipped matches yet to be struck, and a bottle of Visine. The match packet had a caricature picture of Jesus on the cover, with a saying printed below: *Meet my friend Jesus.*

There is one last thing about the cell I was in. The cell door looked like one you might see on *The Andy Griffith Show*, and just outside the cell door was another door, a solid-core door that gave ingress and egress to the cell area where I was confined.

It began loudly. I hollered to the jailer saying, "Bring me some water."

No response.

I yelled again, "Bring me some water."

No answer.

I said, "Please bring me some water."

After the third holler, I heard somebody say, "You will not get any water. I have been trying all night." The voice was coming from my neighbor in the cell next door. I could hear him through the bars affixed atop and spanning our common wall.

My mania bit into his words and made them part of the manic rage that was about to happen. "I will have them bringing water for you and me both," I said back to my neighbor.

He replied, "Good luck."

I called out to the jailer a few more times for water, and then I started raising H-E double hockey sticks. So much so, that the jailer did come, but not with water. He brought with him a can of mace. He threatened me with the mace at first, but within a short minute, my defiant behavior against the jailer produced my standing with my face stuck through the cell door bars, spitting and spewing all sorts of awful language and demeaning slanders toward the jailer.

The jailer obliged by emptying the entire can of mace into my eyes.

I did not flinch. I kept my eyes open entirely, until the can of mace was empty. The chemical ran down my face onto my neck and chest. I don't remember even blinking. Pain did not exist.

When he was through with the mace, I asked him condescendingly with explicitness, "Do you feel like a man now, you blanket-blank-blank?" I am not going to reverb all of the profanity I used in those moments. I shouldn't. Dad-gum is not one of them.

Mace had an effect on me, but it was not a deterrent to getting water. The whites of my eyes were solid blood red for weeks. I took those eyes to Terrell with me. The skin of my face was blistered with the chemical burns. There was a month or two of peeling and healing.

When the jailer left after spraying me with mace, he failed to completely close the solid core door just outside of my cell door. I laid down on the floor, stretched my arms through the bottom of the cell bars to find out that I could touch the solid door with the tips of the three main fingers on my left hand. I presently got hold of the wool blanket from my bed. I struck one of the "close the cover before striking" matches to see if the blanket would burn. The blanket was flame retardant and would not burn, but it did make smoke. I retrieved the Black Cat firecrackers from my hand pocket sweater and twisted four of them together by the fuses. I went to the blanket and started making smoke. When smoke began billowing from the blanket, I laid it near the cell door so the smoke could fill the area in front of my Andy Griffith cell door. I lay down and pushed the solid door open with my fingertips so that smoke could billow into the area where the jailer had his desk. I could not yet see the jailer. Having done this, I stood up, got the firecrackers in hand and hollered, "Fire!" to the top of my lungs.

I could see the jailer coming. I lit the firecrackers and threw them onto the floor outside my cell door.

As soon as the jailer came into the area, the firecrackers began popping. Pop, pop, pop, pop—four of them in quick succession. They made a lot of noise, and a lot of commotion began in the entire jail.

Other county workers came in, but the jailer attending to me, the one who sprayed me with mace, got what my manic mind said he deserved. His eyes were all white, bugged and wide open. He danced a jig, not knowing what to do. He reeled backward against the wall, shuffled his feet, then headed out the door from whence he came.

I blurted out some profanities as he was departing.

The jailer came back with water, but it was in a five-gallon mop bucket to put out the smoldering blanket. It was about midnight, striking New Year's Eve.

The jailer and one other came in and searched my pockets and took my remaining firecrackers and matches. I didn't sleep that night as manics don't need sleep, so we think.

The next day during shift change for the jailers, a nice young man was assigned to me. He brought me a hamburger, French fries, and a Coke for lunch. I started talking to him and actually made friends with him. It had to be true, because at about two o'clock in the afternoon of December 31st, 1984, he drove me to my parents' house in his squad car. You could see the dread and chill in the expressions of my mother and daddy's face and demeanor when they saw me get out of the car. My daddy had told the sheriff's office that under no circumstance do you let Cary John Efurd out of jail. Dad wanted me in jail because he had already completed the paper work to have me committed to TSH. I guess I can say here that there was no communication between staff at the Titus County Jail, or they would definitely not have let me go free.

This is where it ended and started for me. From jail to "L." I was on the road to recovery.

God bless you all, Amen. Cary John Efurd.

Willing to Learn

It is necessary for a mentally ill person, and everyone, to be aware of thoughts. How many times have we heard, "As we think, so we become"?

Our thoughts cause us to gravitate, move and do what we think about. It's just as simple as that. God said it. Not me. God makes things simple, but what he says is sometimes hard to believe. It is a practicing alcoholic's thoughts that keep him inebriated. It is his practice of thinking purely good thoughts that keep him sober. A good thought for an alcoholic may be to get some help. Addiction and sobriety are both the results of thought. Thinking is the action mode of what is in our heart and soul.

If we have regret, we are going to think about regret. If we can recognize regret in our thinking, we can turn it around and think about forgiveness or restitution. We have to get our critical thoughts of failure changed to a successful way of thinking.

Without a clean mind, what do we have? Perhaps depression, suicidal thoughts, and criminal activity could be stated for starters.

In my life, I have done a lot of things for which one could say I only got a slap on the wrist. I don't know what that one would want for me. Whether I was drinking or manic, my mind did not think good, clean, pure thoughts. Even sober and in a stable mental state, I still tinker in negative thinking, but not for long. I have good thoughts to turn to now.

The prayers I write in the morning for my Facebook friends help me. Sometimes it takes as much as two hours to write a few simple lines. All the while, I am in meditation, searching for what God would have me say, which is good for my spiritual development.

You might say, "Cary John, you have a mental illness."

I say, all the more do I need to practice having good, clean, pure thoughts, and do what it needed to take care of myself. I don't want another death on my conscience. God's Word does not condemn. His Word is good for instruction. I go to a Bible study, prayer meetings, AA meetings, and church. I read, study, and pray to get the help. Everyone is the same when it comes to thinking.

Our free will can turn our thoughts to seeking God's will. Thoughts drive our actions and is the most essential thing for mental health in everybody. With good thinking comes good feelings, happiness, and joy. Life looks better. Work is more enjoyable. Our family relationships are better, and when trouble hits, we are more equipped to handle it.

I have made a lot of trouble in my life. I now call it *big trouble*. When I made a decision to turn my will and my life over to the care of God, things started changing. Obedience in one thing leads to obedience in many more things, if our hat is off to God Almighty.

When I started my business in 2005, I was working for wages, pennies on the dollar, you might say, but I was up from $1.11 per hour out of Terrell to $6.50 an hour in 1986, to $11.64 in 1990, to bankrupt in 1998, and then $10.00 an hour in January of 1999.

I told you the story of what tithing did for me. It took me out of focus on the love of money to a focus on God Almighty. One thing led to another until I paid off my bankruptcy, gave up 100 percent of my salary and ended up running and selling a million-dollar business in twelve years. I tell you this for the glory of God in my life. I tried it the other way already. My success proved I could operate seven failed businesses in my own power and ways of thinking.

I can't explain how all of this happened, or prove it. I can only share details. Terrell taught me one thing and drove it home. It was this: "Examine what you are thinking about." Examine, be it regrets, unforgiveness, joy, pleasure, or pain. I call it thinking about what you are thinking about.

You and I may be surprised when we ask ourselves the question: "What am I thinking about right now?"

The short of this story is that I have been filled with gladness and I love everything about my life. God's forgiveness and the court's decisions in my troubles have played in my favor only because it happened that way. Should I regret? I am sorry, but I can't live my life in vain regret. Neither should anybody living.

My wife said to me while I was in depression, "Cary, don't let that boy's life go in vain." She was really saying, do something positive with your experience. I have been telling the stories you have read, to various people and groups for a long while. I remember Gabriel every time I look at my burn-scarred arms and wander through the details of my past.

Below is a prayer I wrote when I opened my real estate business on a shoestring in 2005. I wrote in about as many words as I can type, which is about 40 WPM. I call it my business plan. It came out of me like writing one of these stories sometimes does.

I read parts of it every day. Many times, I read all of it. At my business, it hung near my desk on a wall, the east wall behind me near the door. I'd stop for a few moments coming in each day and read. Sometimes I'd take it to my desk and keep it there to refer to as I was writing an email to a customer or talking with them on the phone. Even while visiting in my office, I could glance. This prayer is my bond to proper thinking. It is my prayer that you will write a prayer for yourself. What comes out of our mind, tells us what we are thinking and where we are headed. Most people want to do what is right. It became a must for me.

Dear Lord,

I am not afraid of anything. I never give up. I esteem other people more than myself. I always go the extra mile in service. I live in hope of a better tomorrow. I am always producing quality action and thought. The elements of love and joy are evident in my life. I am thankful for everything that happens to me.

Criticizing, condemning and complaining are not a part of my psyche. I have a heart for service. Nothing interferes with my desire, willingness, and decision to do the right thing. When I am perplexed, I believe that my faith is established, and I wait with patience to see the answers avail themselves right before my eyes.

I am never, ever in disbelief of good in every person. I can see into the hearts of others and feel their pain.

I do not bind myself in believing that the amount of money I have is the reason for my existence. Others always know that I have their best interest in mind. I go to any length to do my job. I do my work with enthusiasm. I am always looking for ways to do my work better.

I am a marketing wizard. I am a developer and promoter of a large organization. I get up each morning and go to bed every night knowing that I will and have done all that I can do to make life better for those around me—in my home, in my community, and in my world.

I love to do what is right. I live each day with the thoughts of kindness, forgiveness, and generosity. I cast not a downward view on my fellowman.

I look for the good in everyone. I look at the condition of men's hearts, not their outward appearance. I find myself in every way a slave to doing the right thing. I discern easily the matters that require a correct decision.

I believe my family is the better part of my life. I am an encourager, motivator, and highly defined man of character, the kind of character that engages others in trust, confidence, and good works.

I believe good works must be produced with faith, seeking to edify and promote the spiritual domination of good over bad, rather than self-seeking motives. There is never too much to do, nor do I have the inability to get things done. Work and projects are things and are only the results of my actions.

I have the power to accomplish everything that comes my way. I do every task as unto God Almighty, with the hope that I will do everything as his will intends.

I look for guidance through God's Word and the truth in the nature of his people, the ones he has placed in my life to look up to, reach out to, and serve. I believe that I can only serve God by serving people. I never miss an opportunity to be of service. I will that my only will be after the Father of the universe, the guiding force that speaks inside of me, and the meaning of good words that I meditate upon.

When negative thoughts come to my mind, I immediately stop and focus on a good word, a good person, a good place or a good situation. I seek the good! I always have a good word, person, place, and situation to think about.

I believe that my life will always be as God intends. I am willing to accept every situation as being good for me. I believe that I will always be able to escape the snare of bad thinking. Bad thoughts do not haunt me. I do not have bad thoughts as I meditate on what is good. I remain composed and poised at all times.

I never ignore what needs to be done, not even the unpleasant. I believe unpleasant tasks teach character, offer guidance and truth. Therefore, I accept unpleasant tasks as tasks that are good and view them thusly. I look for guidance at every hand, every turn, every bend in the road of my successful life. Success is how I view it. I view my life as success.

Thank you, dear God, for giving me this day my daily bread and for allowing me another opportunity to serve you by serving others. I ask that

when I am wrong that I promptly see it. I ask that I may become
enhanced by quality of character, the kind of character that pleases you
and those around me. I am provoked to wonder when I may find the
kind of character that esteems not me. Please let me know that I am
doing something of what you want me to do. I hope to do it more and
more. I hope to become a true man of character.

In the name of Jesus,
Sincerely and Amen
Cary John Efurd
September 12, 2005

It is necessary for a mentally ill person, and everyone who has difficulties with worrying about the same old things, to be aware of what we are thinking about. Our thinking produces our emotions. Emotions are not facts. Just because we may feel hopeless, unlovable, and worthless doesn't mean that we are. If we want to feel joyful and happy, we must keep our thoughts in check.

The actions that produce our difficulties have already happened, unless we are worried about the future and the future has not happened yet, but we are moving toward the future, second by second. The present has already passed. Our thoughts cause us to gravitate, move to and do what we think about. It's just as simple as that. God gave us feelings and emotions for a reason. Living by faith doesn't mean we ignore our emotions. They are not evil by themselves, but they can cause us to feel like the devil.

It is a practicing alcoholic's thoughts that keep him inebriated. It is his practice of thinking purely good thoughts that keep him sober. A good thought for an alcoholic may be to get some help by changing thought patterns.

Thinking is the action mode of what is in our heart and soul. If we have regret, we are going to think about regret. If we can recognize regret in our thinking, we can turn it around and think about forgiveness or restitution.

We have to get our critical thoughts of failure changed to a successful way of thinking. Without a clean mind, what do we have? Perhaps depression, suicidal thoughts, and criminal activity could be stated for starters. In my life, I have done all of that, because my mind did not think good, clean, pure thoughts.

I still tinker in negative thinking, but not for long. I have good thoughts to turn to now.

You might say, "Cary John, you have a mental illness."

I say, "All the more do I need to practice having good, clean, pure thoughts, and do what it takes to take care of myself." I don't want another death on my conscience.

God's word does not condemn. His word is good for instruction. Everyone is the same when it comes to thinking. Our free will can turn our thoughts to seeking God's will.

Where do we find good thoughts and God's will? In the Bible and through the Holy Spirit's comforting. Thoughts drive our actions and is the most essential thing for mental health, everybody. With good thinking comes good feelings, happiness, and joy. Life looks better. Work is more enjoyable. Our family relationships are better, and when trouble hits, we are more equipped to handle it.

I have made a lot of trouble in my life and some might say I now call it big trouble. When I made a decision to turn my will and my life over to the care of God, things started changing. I can pinpoint when it happened—in August of 2004 when my wife and I started tithing. It was a simple leap of faith in obedience. I have already told you about the $5,000, selling my business. The whole story you have read about tithing. What that simple act did was lead me into more obedience to God's Word. I started looking for ways to do more, better.

In 2005 I started my own brokers firm in real estate.

Do I still have thoughts that lead me down the road to wanting to have another drink? The answer is yes. When I stop at a stop light, for instance, alongside of a truck hauling beer and see the icy sweat drops trickling down the side of a beer can, it does look appealing. When I am with friends and family who drink, I say to myself, *It'd be nice to be able to drink a beer with them.* It's a bonding thing, I reckon, but a can of icy cold Diet Coke does the same thing. I am holding something, and it's in a can. Those who know me don't want me to drink. When I kid about getting drunk, I get bad reviews.

In those times and others, I am quickly drawn by my thoughts, now out of habit, to my past experiences. I remember my last drink which was bourbon (Ezra Brooks). My last drink was a half fifth that I all but guzzled. I remember how it turned out, another eight months in Terrell State Hospital. I don't want to go there, badly. I remember what it was like then and am given reprieve by knowing what it is like now. I have a good solid life. If you have seen the movie *Rudy*, you will know what I mean when I say, it's not so bad being a Rudiger (Efurd). I live on a farm with cows and dogs.

Do I ever have manic delights of grandeur and feelings of invincibility now? The answer is no, but I remember what they were like. These feelings and others are appealing, because they felt so good, but the same answer to alcohol applies to the mental illness of bipolar. From all of the treatment and disasters that happened in my life past, I have learned a thing or three. Number one is: *Don't go there Cary John. Turn your thoughts to what is good and right in the eyes of God.*

Every challenge I face with my mental illness and substance addiction is met with victory because I have a new medicine for my mind that was prescribed to me by the teachings and examples of Jesus Christ, who was made God All Mighty in the flesh. I have the Holy Spirit that speaks to me from the tables of my heart, where I have as much of God's word written as I now have and am seeking to write more.

I cannot quote very many Scripture verses, but I know what the Bible says from reading, study, meditation, listening to sermons, Christian music and Sunday school from as early as I can remember unto now.

Not everybody has this much to work with, but many have more. Everyone has something they can start with, though. It has to do with becoming willing to learn. It only takes a few minutes each day to learn something about what God has to say. I believe finding obedience to continuous meditation and prayer will cause proclamations of joy springing forth in our lives.

Most people want more peace, understanding, and relief from something, be it worry, fear, or grief. These things usually come into play, or stem from one or more of the seven deadly sins of pride, greed, lust, envy, gluttony, wrath, or sloth.

It is said that pride is the sin that leads to the others. I have been full of pride and truly have more of it now than I care to admit. Even a little bit is too much. So I watch out for it in my life.

When anything crops up that troubles me, I can go to the prayer closet of my mind and stay there with Jesus in my heart and get through any so-called crisis. Anyone can. Nothing that we worry about really every happens. It is the things that crop up out of the clear blue that we have to be ready for.

How do we get ready or prepared for a calamity occurrence? I'll call it a calamity, but by being prepared, nothing is ever as bad as it seems. Our fourth-grade teacher may have told us that, or our mother or father, or our friend and family. We have all heard it.

Being prepared in this mind of a very lowly layman of the word of God means taking time to receive the Word of God that has been so generously given. Write it on the tables of our hearts so that it will come to us as needed, which is all the time in actuality, but more-importantly in the times when we need them most. The words in our heart comes to our mind and we apply them in each situation.

The things that happen to us are not just calamities of, say, the death of a close friend or loved one—mother, brother, father, or sister—loss of a job, a car wreck, or sudden life-threatening illness. All of these things feel like trouble when they happen. There is no question. What happens next, after the calamity event occurs? The Believer immediately goes to the Word of God and his grace.

The psychologists that I have talked to offer that there are five stages of grief that we go through for the loss of a loved one. I believe these steps can apply to any calamity we face. They are denial, anger, bargaining, depression, and acceptance. They are called tools to help us identify what we may be feeling. But they are not stops on a linear timeline. In other words, these tools will not stop the pain but are only identifiers of our feelings.

I go back to a story I have shared with you in a past writing. My aunt Joyce answered her grief like this. "I lean." What she meant is that she leans on the everlasting arms of Jesus. Aunt Joyce is ninety-three years old now, and still leaning. I talked to her this afternoon.

Think about it, dear believer. What more could we ask for? Do calamities hurt? Yes, they do. Is God still alive inside us? Yes, he is. Now the subject turns to *how*? It is an attitude of willingness, just the same as when we were first saved. We know Jesus is there, but we want him here with us during a calamity. This is the reason we should always have a prayer on our heart and in our mind.

I wrote a prayer just this morning that said in part, *We can take Jesus with us while taking out the trash or when weeding the garden.* This was an illustration to point out that we have a lot of trash in our minds and weeds in the words we tell ourselves. Prayer and

102

meditation and direct contact with our innermost selves is where the stimulation begins to recover from calamity.

It has been said that Jesus is the only way. How strongly do we apply this truth to our lives, to our calamities? It takes a conscious effort to remain in constant contact with God. He never leaves us. We leave him. That is to say that when we leave him, he is still there.

For unbelievers, this kind of talk is hogwash. Many Christian people have trouble with it too. There is a movie that I really like called *Trouble with the Curve*. Many in calamity have trouble with the Word. Trouble with the Word is a byproduct of trouble getting into the Word. There is not a one of us who worry, grieve, have sorrow, and are sad who shouldn't run to Jesus and his promises for help. Unbelievers too!

Why all of this? I started this story talking about myself and my past. I have talked an awful lot about myself and my past through the entirety of my writings, but the stories are not about me. They are about you and Jesus. I don't like taking about me, but I am my best subject, not my favorite.

There is a way to come out on the other side of calamity. Do what God says. "Come to me, all of you who are heavy laden, overworked in spirit and worried. I will give you rest" (paraphrased). Why would we not take God up on his promise? Just that one scripture verse is enough. It's the practice that becomes a habit to go to him that will cause us to have no more trouble with the Word of God. Amen.

Everlasting to Everlasting

From everlasting to everlasting, the guiding Spirit of Truth, and the wisdom of the ages are steadfast, ever-present and living within each believer in Jesus Christ. For us to tap into this wonderful source of strength and wellspring from which we can quench a parched spirit, we have but to become willing. We must become willing to try.

Fear is a malady of the spirit. It affects our minds. Bad habits cause maladies, such as never having any money, because we overspent freely, not thinking of the future. Drinking and drug abuse cause maladies. Blaming circumstances and other people for our own unfortunate situation are other maladies that can beset us. If our thinking is not clearly focused on the Way, the Truth, and the Light, God's ways, maladies will surely come to live with us.

Greed and jealousy are two more malicious maladies causing illnesses of the mind, heart and soul. A malady can put us at home in the bed sick, the hospital or worse, but will surely cloud our days at a minimum. Malady defined is "bad or ill," "something bad is holding us."

I have been given a lot, so much so that I began to take it all for granted, which turned my thinking into the malady of self-importance. I got sick of me because others got sick of me first. Maladies can blind us from seeing ourselves in the illnesses of our spirit.

As we reflect on our lives, what malady may be holding you right now? Make a list of them in your mind, on paper, or text a note to yourself. It is good to consistently, constantly review our lives for maladies.

Regarding self-importance, it is fuel to the ego, resulting in anger, indifference to others, and the list goes on. Self-importance has to be fed, and often at the expense of others.

I asked Debby, "Why did you stay with me when you had every good reason to leave me?"

She answered, "Because I made a commitment in our marriage vow before God and you." She said this long before I started writing this book. A commitment can turn to malady if it is not kept holy before God.

God committed to us first. We could not know him had he not first known us. When a person accepts Christ as Savior, commitment to him begins. We must go to him with our maladies.

He will never leave us. He can't, because he promised that he would not. We simply must stay the course and remember our commitment and his promises. His rescue of us from troubled times is sure. Let us leave our maladies with Jesus and move bravely on, brothers and sisters in Christ. He is waiting for us.

If you are reading this and do not know of God's plan for salvation, here it is"

- Realize that there is no other place to turn but to another empty malady. Simply stated, realize you are a sinner. Romans 3:23.
- Realize that the payment for sin is death. Romans 6:23.
- Realize that Jesus died on the cross for your sins. Romans 5:8.
- Repent, turn from, your sins, accept Jesus as your Savior, and ask him to come into your life. Romans 10:9.

Lord, may the words of our mouths and the meditations of our hearts be acceptable unto you.

In Jesus name,

Amen.

Made in the USA
Middletown, DE
16 October 2021